ALL NEW! SECRET RESTAURANT ★RECIPES★

Publications International, Ltd.

TABLE OF CONTENTS

APPETIZERS

MEDITERRANEAN BAKED FETA
MAKES 4 TO 6 SERVINGS

1 package (8 ounces) feta cheese, cut crosswise into 4 slices

½ cup grape tomatoes, halved

¼ cup sliced roasted peppers

¼ cup pitted kalamata olives

⅛ teaspoon dried oregano

Black pepper

2 tablespoons extra virgin olive oil

1 tablespoon shredded fresh basil

Pita chips

1 Preheat oven to 400°F.

2 Place cheese in small baking dish; top with tomatoes, roasted peppers and olives. Sprinkle with oregano and season with black pepper; drizzle with oil.

3 Bake 12 minutes or until cheese is soft. Sprinkle with basil. Serve immediately with pita chips.

FRIED MACARONI AND CHEESE BITES
MAKES 48 PIECES (ABOUT 8 SERVINGS)

8 ounces uncooked elbow macaroni

2 tablespoons butter

2 tablespoons all-purpose flour

2 cups milk

1 teaspoon salt, divided

2 cups (8 ounces) shredded Cheddar cheese

1 cup (4 ounces) shredded Swiss cheese

1 cup (4 ounces) shredded smoked Gouda cheese

Vegetable oil for frying

3 eggs

¼ cup water

2 cups plain dry bread crumbs

1 teaspoon Italian seasoning

Marinara sauce, heated

1 Cook macaroni in large saucepan of boiling salted water 7 minutes or until al dente. Drain and set aside.

2 Melt butter in same saucepan over medium-high heat. Whisk in flour until smooth. Cook 1 minute, whisking frequently. Slowly whisk in milk in thin steady stream; cook over medium-high heat about 8 minutes or until thickened. Add ½ teaspoon salt. Gradually stir in cheeses until melted and smooth. Stir in macaroni.

3 Spray 9-inch square baking pan with nonstick cooking spray. Spread macaroni and cheese in prepared pan; smooth top. Cover with plastic wrap; refrigerate 4 hours or until firm and cold.

4 Turn out macaroni and cheese onto cutting board; cut into 48 pieces. Heat ½ inch of oil in large deep skillet or saucepan to 350°F over medium-high heat.

5 Whisk eggs and ¼ cup water in medium bowl. Combine bread crumbs, Italian seasoning and remaining ½ teaspoon salt in another medium bowl. Working with a few pieces at a time, dip macaroni and cheese pieces in egg, then roll in bread crumb mixture to coat. Place on large baking sheet. Dip coated pieces in egg mixture again; roll in bread crumb mixture to coat.

6 Fry in batches about 3 minutes or until deep golden brown, turning once. Remove to paper towel-lined wire rack. Return oil to 350°F between batches. Serve warm with marinara sauce for dipping.

PRETZEL STICKS WITH BEER-CHEESE DIP
MAKES 6 TO 8 SERVINGS

PRETZELS

1⅔ cups warm water (110° to 115°F)

1 package (¼ ounce) active dry yeast

2 teaspoons sugar

1 teaspoon salt

4½ cups all-purpose flour, plus additional for work surface

2 tablespoons butter, softened

2 tablespoons vegetable oil

12 cups water

½ cup baking soda

Kosher salt or pretzel salt and sesame seeds

HONEY-MUSTARD DIP

⅓ cup sour cream

¼ cup Dijon mustard

3 tablespoons honey

BEER-CHEESE DIP

2 tablespoons butter

1 clove garlic, minced

2 tablespoons all-purpose flour

1 tablespoon Dijon mustard

1 teaspoon Worcestershire sauce

1 cup Belgian white ale

2 cups (8 ounces) shredded white Cheddar cheese

1 cup (4 ounces) shredded Monterey Jack cheese

Black pepper (optional)

1 Combine 1⅔ cups warm water, yeast, sugar and 1 teaspoon salt in large bowl of electric stand mixer; stir to dissolve yeast. Let stand 5 minutes or until bubbly. Add 4½ cups flour and softened butter; beat at low speed until combined, scraping side of bowl occasionally. Replace paddle attachment with dough hook; knead at medium-low speed 5 minutes. Place dough in large greased bowl; turn to grease top. Cover and let rise in warm place 1 hour or until doubled in size.

2 For mustard dip, combine sour cream, ¼ cup mustard and honey in small bowl; mix well. Refrigerate until ready to use.

3 Preheat oven to 450°F. Brush 1 tablespoon oil over each of two large baking sheets. Bring 12 cups water to a boil in large saucepan or Dutch oven.

4 Punch down dough; turn out onto floured work surface. Divide dough into 14 equal pieces. Flatten and stretch each piece; roll into 12-inch-long rope. Cut each rope in half.

5 Carefully stir baking soda into boiling water. Working in batches, drop dough pieces into boiling water; cook 30 seconds. Remove to prepared baking sheets with slotted spoon. Make 3 to 4 slashes in each pretzel stick with sharp knife. Sprinkle with coarse salt and sesame seeds.

6 Bake 14 to 15 minutes or until dark golden brown, rotating baking sheets halfway through baking time. Cool slightly on wire rack.

7 Meanwhile for cheese dip, melt 2 tablespoons butter in medium saucepan over medium heat. Add garlic; cook and stir 1 minute. Whisk in 2 tablespoons flour until well blended; cook 1 minute. Whisk in 1 tablespoon mustard and Worcestershire sauce. Slowly whisk in ale in thin steady stream. Cook 1 minute or until slightly thickened. Add cheeses by ¼ cupfuls, stirring until cheeses are melted before adding next addition. Transfer to serving bowl; sprinkle with pepper, if desired. Serve pretzels warm with dips.

APPETIZERS

TEX-MEX NACHOS

MAKES 4 TO 6 SERVINGS

1 tablespoon vegetable oil

8 ounces ground beef

½ cup chopped onion

2 cloves garlic, minced

2 teaspoons chili powder

1 teaspoon ground cumin

½ teaspoon salt

½ teaspoon dried oregano

1 can (about 15 ounces) kidney beans, rinsed and drained

½ cup corn

½ cup sour cream, divided

2 tablespoons mayonnaise

1 tablespoon lime juice

¼ to ½ teaspoon chipotle chili powder

½ bag tortilla chips

½ (15-ounce) jar Cheddar cheese dip, warmed

½ cup pico de gallo

¼ cup guacamole

1 cup shredded iceberg lettuce

2 jalapeño peppers, thinly sliced into rings

1 Heat oil in large skillet over medium-high heat. Add beef, onion and garlic; cook and stir 6 minutes or until beef is no longer pink. Add chili powder, cumin, salt and oregano; cook and stir 1 minute. Add beans and corn; reduce heat to medium-low and cook 3 minutes or until heated through.

2 For chipotle sauce, combine ¼ cup sour cream, mayonnaise, lime juice and chipotle chili powder in small bowl; mix well. Place in small plastic squeeze bottle.

3 Spread tortilla chips on platter or large plate. Top with beef mixture; drizzle with cheese dip. Top with pico de gallo, guacamole, remaining ¼ cup sour cream, lettuce and jalapeños. Squeeze chipotle sauce over nachos. Serve immediately.

PEPPERONI BREAD

MAKES ABOUT 6 SERVINGS

1 container (about 14 ounces) refrigerated pizza dough

8 slices provolone cheese

20 to 30 slices pepperoni (about half of 6-ounce package)

½ teaspoon Italian seasoning

¾ cup (3 ounces) shredded mozzarella cheese

½ cup grated Parmesan cheese

1 egg, beaten

Marinara sauce, heated

1 Preheat oven to 400°F. Unroll pizza dough on sheet of parchment paper with long side in front of you. Cut off corners of dough to create oval shape.

2 Arrange half of provolone slices over bottom half of oval, cutting to fit as necessary. Top with pepperoni; sprinkle with ¼ teaspoon Italian seasoning. Top with mozzarella, Parmesan and remaining provolone slices; sprinkle with remaining Italian seasoning.

3 Fold top half of dough over filling to create half moon (calzone) shape; press edges with fork or pinch edges to seal. Transfer calzone with parchment paper to large baking sheet; curve slightly into crescent shape. Brush with beaten egg.

4 Bake about 16 minutes or until crust is golden brown. Remove to wire rack to cool slightly. Cut crosswise into slices; serve warm with marinara sauce.

CRAB SHACK DIP

MAKES 6 TO 8 SERVINGS (ABOUT 3½ CUPS)

½ (8-ounce) package cream cheese, softened

½ cup sour cream

2 tablespoons mayonnaise

¾ teaspoon seasoned salt

¼ teaspoon paprika, plus additional for garnish

2 cans (6 ounces each) crabmeat, drained and flaked

½ cup (2 ounces) shredded mozzarella cheese

2 tablespoons minced onion

2 tablespoons finely chopped green bell pepper*

Chopped fresh parsley (optional)

Tortilla chips

For a spicier dip, substitute 1 tablespoon minced jalapeño pepper for the bell pepper.

1 Preheat oven to 350°F.

2 Combine cream cheese, sour cream, mayonnaise, seasoned salt and ¼ teaspoon paprika in medium bowl; stir until well blended and smooth. Add crabmeat, cheese, onion and bell pepper; stir until blended. Spread in small (1-quart) shallow baking dish.

3 Bake 15 to 20 minutes or until bubbly and top is beginning to brown. Garnish with additional paprika and parsley; serve with tortilla chips.

ONION RING STACK

MAKES 4 TO 6 SERVINGS (ABOUT 20 ONION RINGS)

1 cup all-purpose flour, divided

½ cup cornmeal

1 teaspoon black pepper

½ teaspoon salt

¼ to ½ teaspoon ground red pepper

1 cup light-colored beer

Rémoulade Sauce (recipe follows) or ranch dressing

Vegetable oil for frying

6 tablespoons cornstarch, divided

2 large sweet onions, cut into ½-inch rings and separated

1 Combine ½ cup flour, cornmeal, black pepper, salt and red pepper in large bowl; mix well. Whisk in beer until well blended. Let stand 1 hour.

2 Prepare rémoulade sauce; refrigerate until ready to serve.

3 Pour oil into large saucepan or Dutch oven to depth of 2 inches; heat to 360°F to 370°F. Line large wire rack with paper towels.

4 Whisk 4 tablespoons cornstarch into batter. Combine remaining ½ cup flour and 2 tablespoons cornstarch in medium bowl. Thoroughly coat onions with flour mixture.

5 Working with one at a time, dip onion rings into batter to coat completely; carefully place in hot oil. Cook about 4 onions rings at a time 3 minutes or until golden brown, turning once. Remove to prepared wire rack; season with additional salt. Return oil to 370°F between batches. Serve immediately with rémoulade sauce.

RÉMOULADE SAUCE

Combine 1 cup mayonnaise, 2 tablespoons coarse-grain mustard, 1 tablespoon lemon juice, 1 tablespoon sweet pickle relish, 1 teaspoon horseradish sauce, 1 teaspoon Worcestershire sauce and ¼ teaspoon hot pepper sauce in medium bowl; mix well.

WHITE SPINACH QUESO

MAKES 4 TO 6 SERVINGS

1 tablespoon olive oil

1 clove garlic, minced

1 tablespoon all-purpose flour

1 can (12 ounces) evaporated milk

½ teaspoon salt

2 cups (8 ounces) shredded Monterey Jack cheese

1 package (10 ounces) frozen chopped spinach, thawed and squeezed dry

Toppings: pico de gallo, guacamole, chopped fresh cilantro and queso fresco

Tortilla chips

1 Preheat broiler.

2 Heat oil in medium saucepan over medium-low heat. Add garlic; cook and stir 1 minute without browning. Add flour; whisk until smooth. Add evaporated milk in thin steady stream, whisking constantly. Stir in salt. Cook about 4 minutes or until slightly thickened, whisking frequently. Add 1½ cups Monterey Jack; whisk until smooth. Stir in spinach. Pour into medium cast iron skillet; sprinkle with remaining ½ cup Monterey Jack.

3 Broil about 1 minute or until cheese is melted and browned in spots. Top with pico de gallo, guacamole, cilantro and queso fresco. Serve immediately with tortilla chips.

FRIED GREEN TOMATOES

MAKES 4 SERVINGS

⅓ cup all-purpose flour

¼ teaspoon salt

2 eggs

1 tablespoon water

½ cup panko bread crumbs

2 large green tomatoes, cut into
   ½-inch-thick slices

½ cup olive oil

½ cup ranch dressing

1 tablespoon sriracha sauce

1 package (5 ounces) spring
   greens salad mix

¼ cup crumbled goat cheese

1 Combine flour and salt in shallow bowl. Beat eggs and water in another shallow bowl. Place panko in third shallow bowl. Coat both sides of tomato slices with flour mixture, shaking off excess. Dip in egg mixture, letting excess drip back into bowl. Roll in panko to coat. Place on plate.

2 Heat oil in large skillet over medium-high heat. Add half of tomato slices, arranging in single layer in skillet. (Cook in two or three batches as necessary; do not overlap.) Cook about 2 minutes per side or until golden brown. Remove to paper towel-lined plate.

3 Combine ranch dressing and sriracha in small bowl; mix well. Divide greens among four serving plates; top with tomatoes. Drizzle with dressing mixture; sprinkle with cheese.

SPINACH FLORENTINE FLATBREAD
MAKES 8 SERVINGS

1 tablespoon olive oil

2 cloves garlic, minced

1 package (10 ounces) baby spinach

1 can (about 14 ounces) quartered artichoke hearts, drained and sliced

½ teaspoon salt

¼ teaspoon dried oregano

Black pepper

Red pepper flakes

2 rectangular pizza or flatbread crusts (about 8 ounces each)

1 plum tomato, seeded and diced

2 cups (8 ounces) shredded Monterey Jack cheese

½ cup (2 ounces) shredded Italian cheese blend

Shredded fresh basil leaves (optional)

1 Preheat oven to 425°F.

2 Heat oil in large nonstick skillet over medium-high heat. Add garlic; cook and stir 30 seconds. Add half of spinach; cook and stir until slightly wilted. Add additional spinach by handfuls; cook about 3 minutes or until completely wilted, stirring occasionally. Transfer to medium bowl; stir in artichokes, salt and oregano. Season with black pepper and red pepper flakes.

3 Place pizza crusts on large baking sheet. Spread spinach mixture over crusts; sprinkle with tomato, Monterey Jack and Italian cheese blend.

4 Bake 12 minutes or until cheeses are melted and edges of crusts are browned. Garnish with basil.

TIP

For crispier crusts, bake flatbreads on a preheated pizza stone or directly on the oven rack.

APPETIZERS

BUFFALO CHICKEN DIP

MAKES 5 CUPS

2 packages (8 ounces each) cream cheese, softened and cut into pieces

1 jar (12 ounces) restaurant-style wing sauce

1 cup ranch dressing

2 cups shredded cooked chicken (from 1 pound boneless skinless chicken breasts)

2 cups (8 ounces) shredded Cheddar cheese

Tortilla chips

Celery sticks

1 Combine cream cheese, wing sauce and ranch dressing in large saucepan; cook over medium-low heat 7 to 10 minutes or until cream cheese is melted and mixture is smooth, whisking frequently.

2 Combine chicken and Cheddar in large bowl. Add cream cheese mixture; stir until well blended. Pour into serving bowl; serve warm with tortilla chips and celery sticks.

PEPPERONI STUFFED MUSHROOMS

MAKES 4 TO 6 SERVINGS

16 medium mushrooms

1 tablespoon olive oil

½ cup finely chopped onion

2 ounces pepperoni, finely chopped (about ½ cup)

¼ cup finely chopped green bell pepper

½ teaspoon seasoned salt

¼ teaspoon dried oregano

⅛ teaspoon black pepper

½ cup crushed buttery crackers (about 12)

¼ cup grated Parmesan cheese

1 tablespoon chopped fresh parsley, plus additional for garnish

1 Preheat oven to 350°F. Line baking sheet with foil; spray foil with nonstick cooking spray.

2 Clean mushrooms; remove stems and set aside caps. Finely chop stems.

3 Heat oil in large skillet over medium-high heat. Add onion; cook and stir 2 to 3 minutes or until softened. Add mushroom stems, pepperoni, bell pepper, seasoned salt, oregano and black pepper; cook and stir about 5 minutes or until vegetables are tender but not browned.

4 Remove from heat; stir in crushed crackers, cheese and 1 tablespoon parsley until blended. Spoon mixture into mushroom caps, mounding slightly in centers. Place filled caps on prepared baking sheet.

5 Bake about 20 minutes or until heated through. Garnish with additional parsley.

ZUCCHINI FRITTE

MAKES 4 SERVINGS

Lemon Aioli (recipe follows)

Vegetable oil for frying

¾ to 1 cup soda water

½ cup all-purpose flour

¼ cup cornstarch

½ teaspoon coarse salt

¼ teaspoon garlic powder

¼ teaspoon dried oregano

¼ teaspoon black pepper

3 cups panko bread crumbs

1½ pounds medium zucchini (6 to 8 inches long), ends trimmed, cut lengthwise into ¼-inch-thick slices

¼ cup grated Parmesan or Romano cheese

Chopped fresh parsley

Lemon wedges

1 Prepare aioli; refrigerate until ready to use.

2 Line baking sheet with paper towels; set aside. Pour oil into large saucepan or Dutch oven to depth of 2 inches; heat to 350°F over medium-high heat.

3 Meanwhile, pour ¾ cup soda water into large bowl. Combine flour, cornstarch, salt, garlic powder, oregano and pepper in small bowl; mix well. Slowly whisk flour mixture into soda water just until blended. Add additional soda water if necessary to reach consistency of thin pancake batter. Place panko in medium bowl.

4 Working with one at a time, dip zucchini slices in batter to coat; let excess batter drip back into bowl. Add to bowl with panko; press panko into zucchini slices to coat both sides completely. Place zucchini on plate.

5 Fry zucchini in batches 3 to 4 minutes or until golden brown. (Return oil to 350°F between batches.) Drain on prepared baking sheet. Sprinkle with cheese and parsley. Serve with aioli and lemon wedges.

LEMON AIOLI

Combine ½ cup mayonnaise, 2 tablespoons lemon juice, 1 tablespoon chopped fresh Italian parsley and 1 teaspoon minced garlic in small bowl; mix well. Season with salt and pepper.

APPETIZERS

SOUPS

CREAMY TOMATO SOUP
MAKES 6 SERVINGS

3 tablespoons olive oil, divided

2 tablespoons butter

1 large onion, finely chopped

2 cloves garlic, minced

2 teaspoons sugar

1 teaspoon salt

½ teaspoon dried oregano

2 cans (28 ounces each) peeled Italian plum tomatoes, undrained

4 cups ½-inch focaccia cubes (half of 9-ounce loaf)

½ teaspoon black pepper

½ cup whipping cream

1 Heat 2 tablespoons oil and butter in large saucepan over medium-high heat. Add onion; cook and stir 5 minutes or until softened. Add garlic, sugar, salt and oregano; cook 30 seconds. Stir in tomatoes with juice; bring to a boil. Reduce heat to medium-low; simmer 45 minutes, stirring occasionally.

2 Meanwhile, prepare croutons. Preheat oven to 350°F. Combine focaccia cubes, remaining 1 tablespoon oil and pepper in large bowl; toss to coat. Spread on rimmed baking sheet. Bake about 10 minutes or until bread is golden brown.

3 Blend soup with immersion blender until smooth (or process in batches in food processor or blender). Stir in cream; cook until heated through. Serve soup topped with croutons.

BEEF VEGETABLE SOUP

MAKES 6 TO 8 SERVINGS

1½ pounds cubed beef stew meat

¼ cup all-purpose flour

3 tablespoons vegetable oil, divided

1 onion, chopped

2 stalks celery, chopped

3 tablespoons tomato paste

2 teaspoons salt

1 teaspoon dried thyme

½ teaspoon garlic powder

¼ teaspoon black pepper

6 cups beef broth, divided

1 can (28 ounces) stewed tomatoes, undrained

1 tablespoon Worcestershire sauce

1 bay leaf

4 red potatoes (about 1 pound), cut into 1-inch pieces

3 medium carrots, cut in half lengthwise then cut into ½-inch slices

6 ounces green beans, trimmed and cut into 1-inch pieces

1 cup frozen corn

1 Combine beef and flour in medium bowl; toss to coat. Heat 1 tablespoon oil in large saucepan or Dutch oven over medium-high heat. Cook beef in two batches about 5 minutes or until browned on all sides, adding additional 1 tablespoon oil after first batch. Transfer beef to medium bowl.

2 Heat remaining 1 tablespoon oil in same saucepan. Add onion and celery; cook and stir about 5 minutes or until softened. Add tomato paste, 2 teaspoons salt, thyme, garlic powder and ¼ teaspoon pepper; cook and stir 1 minute. Stir in 1 cup broth, scraping up any browned bits from bottom of saucepan. Stir in remaining 5 cups broth, tomatoes, Worcestershire sauce, bay leaf and beef; bring to a boil.

3 Reduce heat to low; cover and cook 1 hour and 20 minutes. Add potatoes and carrots; cook 15 minutes. Add green beans and corn; cook 15 minutes or until vegetables are tender. Remove and discard bay leaf. Season with additional salt and pepper.

VEGETARIAN CHILI

MAKES 8 TO 10 SERVINGS

2 tablespoons olive oil

1 onion, finely chopped

2 medium carrots, chopped

1 red bell pepper, chopped

3 tablespoons chili powder

2 tablespoons ground cumin

2 tablespoons tomato paste

2 tablespoons packed dark brown sugar

3 cloves garlic, minced

1 tablespoon dried oregano

1 teaspoon salt

1 can (28 ounces) diced tomatoes

1 can (15 ounces) tomato sauce

1 can (about 15 ounces) small white beans, rinsed and drained

1 can (about 15 ounces) light kidney beans, rinsed and drained

1 can (about 15 ounces) dark kidney beans, rinsed and drained

1 can (about 15 ounces) pinto beans, rinsed and drained

1 cup vegetable broth

1 can (4 ounces) diced mild green chiles

1 ounce unsweetened baking chocolate, chopped

1 tablespoon cider vinegar

1 Heat oil in large saucepan or Dutch oven over medium-high heat. Add onion, carrots and bell pepper; cook 10 minutes or until vegetables are tender, stirring frequently. Add chili powder, cumin, tomato paste, brown sugar, garlic, oregano and salt; cook and stir 1 minute.

2 Stir in tomatoes, tomato sauce, beans, broth, chiles and chocolate; bring to a boil. Reduce heat to medium; cook 20 minutes, stirring occasionally. Stir in vinegar.

HARVEST PUMPKIN SOUP

MAKES 8 SERVINGS

1 sugar pumpkin or acorn squash
(about 2 pounds)

1 kabocha or butternut squash
(about 2 pounds)

Salt and black pepper

2 tablespoons olive oil

2 tablespoons butter

1 large onion, finely chopped

2 stalks celery, chopped

1 medium carrot, chopped

¼ cup packed brown sugar

2 tablespoons tomato paste

1 tablespoon minced fresh ginger

1 clove garlic, minced

1 teaspoon salt

1 teaspoon ground cinnamon

¼ teaspoon ground cumin

¼ teaspoon black pepper

4 cups vegetable broth

1 cup milk

2 teaspoons lemon juice

Roasted pumpkin seeds
(optional, see Tip)

1 Preheat oven to 400°F. Line large baking sheet with foil; spray with nonstick cooking spray.

2 Cut pumpkin and kabocha squash in half; scoop out seeds and strings. Season cut sides with salt and pepper. Place squash cut sides down on prepared baking sheet; bake 30 to 45 minutes or until fork-tender. When squash are cool enough to handle, remove skin; chop flesh into 1-inch pieces.

3 Heat oil and butter in large saucepan or Dutch oven over medium-high heat. Add onion, celery and carrot; cook and stir 5 minutes or until vegetables are tender. Add brown sugar, tomato paste, ginger, garlic, 1 teaspoon salt, cinnamon, cumin and ¼ teaspoon pepper; cook and stir 1 minute. Stir in broth and squash; bring to a boil. Reduce heat to medium; cook 20 minutes or until squash is very soft.

4 Blend soup with immersion blender until desired consistency. (Or process in batches in food processor or blender.) Stir in milk and lemon juice; cook until heated through. Garnish with pumpkin seeds.

TIP

Roasted pumpkin seeds can be found at many supermarkets, or you can roast the seeds that you remove from the pumpkin (and the squash) in the recipe. Combine the seeds with 2 teaspoons vegetable oil and ⅛ teaspoon salt in a small bowl; toss to coat. Spread in a single layer on a small foil-lined baking sheet; bake at 300°F 20 to 25 minutes or until the seeds begin to brown, stirring once.

SOUPS

PEPPERY SICILIAN CHICKEN SOUP

MAKES 8 TO 10 SERVINGS

2 tablespoons olive oil

1 onion, chopped

1 green bell pepper, chopped

3 stalks celery, chopped

3 carrots, chopped

3 cloves garlic, minced

1 tablespoon salt

3 containers (32 ounces each) chicken broth

2 pounds boneless skinless chicken breasts

1 can (28 ounces) diced tomatoes

2 baking potatoes, peeled and cut into ¼-inch pieces

1½ teaspoons ground white pepper*

1½ teaspoons ground black pepper

½ cup chopped fresh parsley

8 ounces uncooked ditalini pasta

Or substitute additional black pepper for the white pepper.

1 Heat oil in large saucepan or Dutch oven over medium heat. Stir in onion, bell pepper, celery and carrots. Reduce heat to medium-low; cover and cook 10 to 15 minutes or until vegetables are tender but not browned, stirring occasionally. Stir in garlic and 1 tablespoon salt; cover and cook 5 minutes.

2 Stir in broth, chicken, tomatoes, potatoes, white pepper and black pepper; bring to a boil. Reduce heat to low; cover and cook 1 hour. Remove chicken to plate; set aside until cool enough to handle. Shred chicken and return to saucepan with parsley.

3 Meanwhile, cook pasta in large saucepan of boiling salted water 7 minutes (or 1 minute less than package directs for al dente). Drain pasta and add to soup. Taste and add additional salt, if desired.

GARDEN VEGETABLE SOUP
MAKES 8 TO 10 SERVINGS

1 tablespoon olive oil

1 medium onion, chopped

1 carrot, chopped

1 stalk celery, chopped

1 medium zucchini, diced

1 medium yellow squash, diced

1 red bell pepper, diced

2 tablespoons tomato paste

2 cloves garlic, minced

2 teaspoons salt

1 teaspoon Italian seasoning

½ teaspoon black pepper

8 cups vegetable broth

1 can (28 ounces) whole tomatoes, chopped, juice reserved

½ cup uncooked pearled barley

1 cup cut green beans (1-inch pieces)

½ cup corn

¼ cup slivered fresh basil

1 tablespoon lemon juice

1 Heat oil in large saucepan or Dutch oven over medium-high heat. Add onion, carrot and celery; cook and stir 8 minutes or until vegetables are softened. Add zucchini, yellow squash and bell pepper; cook and stir 5 minutes or until softened. Stir in tomato paste, garlic, salt, Italian seasoning and black pepper; cook 1 minute.

2 Stir in broth and tomatoes with juice; bring to a boil. Stir in barley. Reduce heat to low; cook 30 minutes. Stir in green beans and corn; cook about 15 minutes or until barley is tender and green beans are crisp-tender. Stir in basil and lemon juice.

ITALIAN WEDDING SOUP

MAKES 8 SERVINGS (14 CUPS)

MEATBALLS

- 2 eggs
- 2 cloves garlic, minced
- 1 teaspoon salt
- ⅛ teaspoon black pepper
- 1½ pounds meat loaf mix (ground beef and pork)
- ¾ cup plain dry bread crumbs
- ½ cup grated Parmesan cheese

SOUP

- 2 tablespoons olive oil
- 1 onion, chopped
- 2 carrots, chopped
- 4 cloves garlic, minced
- 2 heads escarole or curly endive, coarsely chopped
- 8 cups chicken broth
- 1 can (about 14 ounces) Italian plum tomatoes, coarsely chopped, juice reserved
- 3 fresh thyme sprigs
- 1 teaspoon salt
- ½ teaspoon red pepper flakes
- 1 cup uncooked acini di pepe pasta

1 Whisk eggs, 2 cloves garlic, 1 teaspoon salt and black pepper in large bowl until blended. Stir in meat loaf mix, bread crumbs and cheese; mix gently until well blended. Shape mixture by tablespoonfuls into 1-inch balls.

2 Heat oil in large saucepan or Dutch oven over medium heat. Cook meatballs in batches about 5 minutes or until browned. Remove to plate; set aside.

3 Add onion, carrots and 4 cloves garlic to saucepan; cook and stir about 5 minutes or until onion is lightly browned. Add escarole; cook 2 minutes or until wilted. Stir in broth, tomatoes, thyme, 1 teaspoon salt and red pepper flakes; bring to a boil over high heat. Reduce heat to medium-low; cook 15 minutes.

4 Add meatballs and pasta to soup; return to a boil over high heat. Reduce heat to medium; cook 10 minutes or until pasta is tender. Remove thyme sprigs before serving.

LENTIL SOUP

MAKES 6 TO 8 SERVINGS

2 tablespoons olive oil, divided

2 medium onions, chopped

1½ teaspoons salt

4 cloves garlic, minced

¼ cup tomato paste

1 teaspoon dried oregano

½ teaspoon dried basil

¼ teaspoon dried thyme

¼ teaspoon black pepper

½ cup dry sherry or white wine

8 cups vegetable broth

2 cups water

3 carrots, cut into ½-inch pieces

2 cups dried lentils, rinsed and sorted

1 cup chopped fresh parsley

1 tablespoon balsamic vinegar

1 Heat 1 tablespoon oil in large saucepan or Dutch oven over medium heat. Add onions; cook 10 minutes, stirring occasionally. Add remaining 1 tablespoon oil and salt; cook 10 minutes or until onions are golden brown, stirring frequently.

2 Add garlic; cook and stir 1 minute. Add tomato paste, oregano, basil, thyme and pepper; cook and stir 1 minute. Add sherry; cook and stir 30 seconds, scraping up any browned bits from bottom of saucepan.

3 Stir in broth, water, carrots and lentils; cover and bring to a boil over high heat. Reduce heat to medium-low; cook, partially covered, 30 minutes or until lentils are tender.

4 Remove from heat; stir in parsley and vinegar.

CLASSIC FRENCH ONION SOUP

MAKES 4 SERVINGS

3 tablespoons butter

3 large yellow onions
   (about 2 pounds), sliced

3 cans (about 14 ounces each)
   beef broth

½ cup dry sherry

½ teaspoon salt

½ teaspoon dried thyme

¼ teaspoon white pepper

4 slices French bread

1 cup (4 ounces) shredded
   Swiss cheese

1 Melt butter in large saucepan or Dutch oven over medium-high heat. Add onions, cook 15 minutes or until lightly browned, stirring occasionally. Reduce heat to medium; cook 30 to 40 minutes or until onions are deep golden brown, stirring occasionally.

2 Stir in broth, sherry, salt, thyme and pepper; bring to a boil. Reduce heat to low; cook 20 minutes. Preheat broiler.

3 Ladle soup into four heatproof bowls; top with bread slices and cheese. Broil 4 inches from heat 2 to 3 minutes or until cheese is bubbly and browned.

SAUSAGE RICE SOUP

MAKES 4 TO 6 SERVINGS

2 teaspoons olive oil

8 ounces Italian sausage, casings removed

1 small onion, chopped

½ teaspoon fennel seeds

1 tablespoon tomato paste

4 cups chicken broth

1 can (about 14 ounces) whole tomatoes, chopped, juice reserved

1½ cups water

½ cup uncooked rice

¼ teaspoon salt

⅛ teaspoon black pepper

2 to 3 ounces baby spinach

⅓ cup shredded mozzarella cheese

1 Heat oil in large saucepan or Dutch oven over medium-high heat. Add sausage; cook about 8 minutes or until browned, breaking up meat into bite-sized pieces. Add onion; cook and stir 5 minutes or until softened. Add fennel seeds; cook and stir 30 seconds. Add tomato paste; cook and stir 1 minute.

2 Stir in broth, tomatoes with juice, water, rice, ¼ teaspoon salt and ⅛ teaspoon pepper; bring to a boil. Reduce heat to medium-low; cook about 18 minutes or until rice is tender. Stir in spinach; cook 3 minutes or until wilted. Season with additional salt and pepper.

3 Sprinkle with cheese just before serving.

HOT AND SOUR SOUP

MAKES 4 TO 6 SERVINGS

1 package (1 ounce) dried shiitake mushrooms

4 ounces firm tofu, drained

4 cups chicken broth

3 tablespoons white vinegar

2 tablespoons soy sauce

½ to 1 teaspoon hot chili oil

1 teaspoon white pepper, divided

1 cup shredded cooked chicken

½ cup drained canned bamboo shoots, cut into thin strips

3 tablespoons water

2 tablespoons cornstarch

1 egg white, lightly beaten

2 tablespoons balsamic vinegar

1 teaspoon dark sesame oil

¼ cup thinly sliced green onions (optional)

1 Place mushrooms in small bowl; cover with warm water and let stand 20 minutes to soften. Drain mushrooms; squeeze out excess water. Discard stems; slice caps. Press tofu lightly between paper towels; cut into ½-inch cubes.

2 Combine broth, white vinegar, soy sauce, chili oil and ½ teaspoon white pepper in large saucepan; bring to a boil over high heat. Reduce heat to medium-low; cook 2 minutes. Add mushrooms, tofu, chicken and bamboo shoots; cook and stir 5 minutes or until heated through.

3 Stir water into cornstarch in small bowl until smooth. Whisk into soup; cook 4 minutes or until soup boils and thickens, stirring frequently.

4 Remove from heat. Stirring constantly in one direction, slowly pour egg white in thin stream into soup. Stir in balsamic vinegar, sesame oil and remaining ½ teaspoon white pepper. Garnish with green onions.

SALADS

TOMATO WATERMELON SALAD
MAKES 4 SERVINGS

¼ cup extra virgin olive oil

2 tablespoons fresh lemon juice

½ teaspoon honey

½ teaspoon salt

⅛ teaspoon black pepper

2 large heirloom tomatoes
(about 10 ounces each),
cut into 6 slices each

2 cups cubed watermelon
(about 12 ounces)

¼ cup thinly sliced red onion rings

¼ cup crumbled feta cheese

Fresh chervil or parsley sprigs
(optional)

1 Whisk oil, lemon juice, honey, salt and pepper in small bowl until well blended.

2 Arrange tomato slices on four salad plates. Top with watermelon and onion; sprinkle with cheese. Drizzle with dressing; garnish with chervil.

STRAWBERRY FIELDS SALAD

MAKES 4 SERVINGS

GLAZED WALNUTS

2 tablespoons butter

6 tablespoons sugar

1 tablespoon honey

½ teaspoon salt

⅛ teaspoon ground red pepper

1 cup walnuts

DRESSING

1 cup fresh strawberries, hulled

½ cup vegetable oil

6 tablespoons white wine vinegar

3 tablespoons sugar

3 tablespoons honey

2 tablespoons balsamic vinegar

2 teaspoons Dijon mustard

½ teaspoon dried oregano

¼ teaspoon salt

SALAD

4 cups chopped romaine lettuce

4 cups coarsely chopped fresh spinach

1 cup sliced fresh strawberries

½ cup crumbled feta cheese

2 cups warm cooked chicken slices (about half of a rotisserie chicken)

1 For walnuts, preheat oven to 350°F. Line baking sheet with foil; spray with nonstick cooking spray.

2 Melt butter in medium skillet over medium-high heat. Stir in 6 tablespoons sugar, 1 tablespoon honey, ½ teaspoon salt and red pepper until well blended. Add walnuts; cook 3 minutes or until nuts are glazed and begin to brown, stirring occasionally. Spread in single layer on prepared baking sheet. Bake 7 minutes or until nuts are lightly browned and fragrant. Cook completely on baking sheet. Break into individual nuts.

3 For dressing, combine whole strawberries, oil, white wine vinegar, 3 tablespoons sugar, 3 tablespoons honey, balsamic vinegar, mustard, oregano and ¼ teaspoon salt in blender or food processor; blend 30 seconds or until smooth.

4 For each salad, combine 1 cup lettuce and 1 cup spinach on serving plate. Top with ¼ cup sliced strawberries, ¼ cup glazed walnuts and 2 tablespoons cheese. Drizzle with 2 tablespoons dressing; top with chicken.

GREEN GODDESS COBB SALAD

MAKES 4 SERVINGS

PICKLED ONION

- 1 cup thinly sliced red onion
- ½ cup white wine vinegar
- ¼ cup water
- 2 teaspoons sugar
- 1 teaspoon salt

DRESSING

- 1 cup mayonnaise
- 1 cup fresh Italian parsley leaves
- 1 cup baby arugula
- ¼ cup extra virgin olive oil
- 3 tablespoons lemon juice
- 3 tablespoons minced fresh chives
- 2 tablespoons fresh tarragon leaves

- 1 clove garlic, minced
- 1 teaspoon Dijon mustard
- ½ teaspoon salt
- ⅛ teaspoon black pepper

SALAD

- 4 eggs
- 4 cups Italian salad blend (romaine and radicchio)
- 2 cups chopped stemmed kale
- 2 cups baby arugula
- 2 avocados, sliced and halved
- 2 tomatoes, cut into wedges
- 2 cups cooked chicken strips
- 1 cup chopped crisp-cooked bacon

1 For pickled onion, combine onion, vinegar, ¼ cup water, sugar and 1 teaspoon salt in large glass jar. Seal jar; shake well. Refrigerate at least 1 hour or up to 1 week.

2 For dressing, combine mayonnaise, parsley, 1 cup arugula, oil, lemon juice, chives, tarragon, garlic, mustard, ½ teaspoon salt and pepper in blender or food processor; blend until smooth, stopping to scrape down side once or twice. Transfer to jar; refrigerate until ready to use. Just before serving, thin dressing with 1 to 2 tablespoons water, if necessary, to reach desired consistency.

3 Fill medium saucepan with water; bring to a boil over high heat. Carefully lower eggs into water. Reduce heat to medium; boil gently 12 minutes. Drain eggs; add cold water and ice cubes to saucepan to cool eggs. When eggs are cool enough to handle, peel and cut in half lengthwise.

4 For salad, combine salad blend, kale, 2 cups arugula and pickled onion in large bowl; divide among four individual serving bowls. Top each salad with avocados, tomatoes, chicken, bacon and two egg halves. Drizzle with ¼ cup dressing; toss to coat.

SALADS

CRUNCHY THAI SALAD

MAKES 6 SERVINGS

CHICKEN

- 2 pounds boneless skinless chicken breasts
- 2 tablespoons olive oil
- 2 tablespoons minced garlic
- 1 tablespoon soy sauce
- 1½ teaspoons salt

CILANTRO-LIME DRESSING

- 1 cup loosely packed fresh cilantro leaves
- ½ cup vegetable oil
- ¼ cup coarsely chopped red bell pepper
- 2 tablespoons honey
- 2 tablespoons white vinegar
- 2 tablespoons lime juice
- 2 teaspoons Dijon mustard
- 1 teaspoon dark sesame oil
- 2 teaspoons minced fresh ginger
- 1 teaspoon salt
- ¼ teaspoon black pepper

THAI PEANUT DRESSING

- ¼ cup creamy peanut butter
- 2 tablespoons hot water
- 2 tablespoons seasoned rice vinegar

- 2 tablespoons vegetable oil
- 2 tablespoons honey
- 2 tablespoons packed brown sugar
- 4 teaspoons soy sauce
- ½ teaspoon salt
- ¼ teaspoon ground red pepper

SALAD

- Vegetable oil for frying
- 2 bundles cellophane (bean thread) noodles (about 2 ounces)
- ½ (12-ounce) package wonton wrappers, cut into ½-inch strips
- 1 small head napa cabbage, separated into leaves, halved lengthwise and cut into ¼-inch strips
- 1 small head red cabbage, cut into wedges, cored and cut into ¼-inch strips
- 1 cup shredded carrots
- 1 bunch green onions, thinly sliced
- 1 large seedless cucumber, peeled and julienned
- ½ cup chopped fresh cilantro
- 2 cups shelled edamame (thawed if frozen)
- 1½ cups dry roasted peanuts
- 2 avocados, diced

1 For chicken, preheat oven to 350°F. Line baking sheet with foil. Pound chicken to ½-inch thickness between sheets of plastic wrap. Whisk olive oil, garlic, 1 tablespoon soy sauce and 1½ teaspoons salt in small bowl; rub mixture all over chicken. Place chicken on baking sheet; bake about 20 minutes or until no longer pink in center.

2 For cilantro dressing, combine 1 cup cilantro, ½ cup vegetable oil, bell pepper, 2 tablespoons honey, white vinegar, lime juice, mustard, sesame oil, ginger, 1 teaspoon salt and black pepper in blender; blend until smooth.

3 For peanut dressing, whisk peanut butter, hot water, rice vinegar, 2 tablespoons vegetable oil, 2 tablespoons honey, brown sugar, 4 teaspoons soy sauce, ½ teaspoon salt and red pepper in small bowl until well blended.

4 Pour vegetable oil into large saucepan to depth of 2 inches; heat over medium-high heat to 375°F. Fry cellophane noodles 5 seconds or until puffed, turning once. Drain on paper towel-lined plate. Use same oil to fry wonton strips in batches 1 to 2 minutes or until lightly browned, stirring occasionally to brown all sides. Drain on paper towel-lined plate.

5 Combine napa cabbage, red cabbage, carrots, green onions, cucumber, ½ cup chopped cilantro, edamame and peanuts in large bowl. Add cilantro dressing; toss to coat. Add chicken; stir gently to coat. Divide salad among serving plates; top with fried cellophane noodles, fried wontons and avocado. Drizzle with peanut dressing.

SALADS

MEDITERRANEAN SALAD

MAKES 4 SERVINGS

2 cups chopped iceberg lettuce

2 cups baby spinach

2 cups diced cucumbers

1 cup diced cooked chicken

1 cup chopped roasted red peppers

1 cup grape tomatoes, halved

1 cup quartered artichoke hearts

¾ cup crumbled feta cheese

½ cup chopped red onion

1 cup hummus

½ teaspoon Italian seasoning

1 Divide lettuce and spinach among four salad bowls or plates; top with cucumbers, chicken, roasted peppers, tomatoes, artichokes, cheese and onion.

2 Top salad with hummus; sprinkle with Italian seasoning.

SUPERFOOD KALE SALAD

MAKES 4 SERVINGS

MAPLE-ROASTED CARROTS

8 carrots, trimmed

2 tablespoons maple syrup

2 tablespoons olive oil

½ teaspoon salt

⅛ teaspoon black pepper

Dash ground red pepper

MAPLE-LEMON VINAIGRETTE

¼ cup olive oil

2 tablespoons maple syrup

3 tablespoons lemon juice

¾ teaspoon grated lemon peel

½ teaspoon salt

⅛ teaspoon black pepper

SALAD

4 cups chopped kale

2 cups chopped mixed greens

1 cup dried cranberries

1 cup slivered almonds, toasted*

1 cup shredded Parmesan cheese

1 package (16 ounces) roasted or grilled chicken strips

To toast almonds, spread on ungreased baking sheet. Bake in preheated 350°F oven 6 to 8 minutes or until lightly browned, stirring occasionally.

1 Preheat oven to 400°F. Line baking sheet with parchment paper. Spray 13×9-inch baking pan with nonstick cooking spray.

2 Place carrots on prepared baking sheet. Whisk 2 tablespoons maple syrup, 2 tablespoons oil, ½ teaspoon salt, ⅛ teaspoon black pepper and red pepper in small bowl until well blended. Brush some of oil mixture over carrots. Roast 30 minutes or until carrots are tender, brushing with oil mixture and shaking pan every 10 minutes. Slice crosswise into coins when carrots are cool enough to handle.

3 While carrots are roasting, prepare vinaigrette. Whisk ¼ cup oil, 2 tablespoons maple syrup, lemon juice, lemon peel, ½ teaspoon salt and ⅛ teaspoon black pepper in small bowl until well blended.

4 For salad, combine kale, greens, cranberries, almonds and cheese in large bowl. Add carrots. Pour vinaigrette over salad; toss to coat. Top with chicken.

TACO SALAD SUPREME
MAKES 4 SERVINGS

CHILI

- 1 pound ground beef
- 1 medium onion, chopped
- 1 stalk celery, chopped
- 2 medium tomatoes, chopped
- 1 jalapeño pepper, finely chopped
- 1½ teaspoons chili powder
- 1 teaspoon salt
- 1 teaspoon ground cumin
- ½ teaspoon black pepper
- 1 can (15 ounces) tomato sauce
- 1 can (about 15 ounces) kidney beans, rinsed and drained
- 1 can (about 15 ounces) pinto beans, rinsed and drained
- 1 cup water

SALAD

- 8 cups chopped romaine lettuce (large pieces)
- 2 cups diced fresh tomatoes
- 48 small round tortilla chips
- 1 cup salsa
- ½ cup sour cream
- 1 cup (4 ounces) shredded Cheddar cheese

1 For chili, combine beef, onion and celery in large saucepan; cook over medium-high heat 6 to 8 minutes or until beef is no longer pink, stirring to break up meat. Drain fat.

2 Add tomatoes, jalapeño, chili powder, salt, cumin and black pepper; cook and stir 1 minute. Stir in tomato sauce, beans and water; bring to a boil. Reduce heat to medium-low; cook about 1 hour or until most of liquid is absorbed.

3 For each salad, combine 2 cups lettuce and ½ cup diced tomatoes in individual serving bowl. Top with 12 tortilla chips, ¾ cup chili, ¼ cup salsa and 2 tablespoons sour cream. Sprinkle with ¼ cup cheese. (Reserve remaining chili for another use.)

ASPARAGUS AND ARUGULA SALAD
MAKE 4 TO 6 SERVINGS

½ cup sun-dried tomatoes
   (not packed in oil)

1 cup boiling water

1 cup sliced asparagus
   (1-inch pieces)

1 package (5 ounces) baby arugula
   (4 cups)

½ cup shaved Parmesan cheese

¼ cup extra virgin olive oil

2 tablespoons lemon juice

1 tablespoon orange juice

1 clove garlic, minced

½ teaspoon salt

½ teaspoon grated lemon peel

⅛ teaspoon black pepper (optional)

1 Place sun-dried tomatoes in small bowl; pour boiling water over tomatoes. Let stand 5 minutes; drain well.

2 Bring medium saucepan of salted water to a boil. Add asparagus; cook 1 minute or until crisp-tender. Rinse under cold running water to stop cooking.

3 Combine arugula, asparagus, sun-dried tomatoes and cheese in large bowl. Whisk oil, lemon juice, orange juice, garlic, salt, lemon peel and pepper, if desired, in small bowl until well blended. Pour over salad; toss gently to coat.

AUTUMN HARVEST SALAD
MAKES 6 SERVINGS

DRESSING

½ cup extra virgin olive oil

3 tablespoons balsamic vinegar

1 clove garlic, minced

1 teaspoon honey

1 teaspoon Dijon mustard

½ teaspoon dried oregano

½ teaspoon salt

⅛ teaspoon black pepper

SALAD

1 loaf (12 to 16 ounces) artisan pecan raisin bread

4 tablespoons (½ stick) butter, melted

6 tablespoons coarse sugar (such as demerara, turbinado or organic cane sugar)

6 cups packed spring greens

2 Granny Smith apples, thinly sliced

1 package (9 ounces) grilled chicken strips

¾ cup crumbled blue cheese

¾ cup dried cranberries

¾ cup walnuts

1 For dressing, whisk oil, vinegar, garlic, honey, mustard, oregano, salt and pepper in medium bowl until well blended.

2 Preheat oven to 350°F. Line baking sheet with parchment paper. Cut bread into thin (¼-inch) slices; place in single layer on prepared baking sheet. Brush one side of each slice with melted butter; sprinkle each slice with ½ teaspoon sugar. Bake 10 minutes. Turn slices; brush other side with butter and sprinkle with ½ teaspoon sugar. Bake 10 minutes. Cool completely on baking sheet.

3 For each salad, place 1 cup greens on serving plate. Top with ½ cup apple slices, ¼ cup chicken strips and 2 tablespoons *each* cheese, cranberries and walnuts. Break 2 slices of toast into pieces and arrange on salad. Drizzle with 2 tablespoons dressing.

SPINACH SALAD

MAKES 4 SERVINGS

DRESSING

- ¼ cup balsamic vinegar
- 1 clove garlic, minced
- ½ teaspoon sugar
- ¼ teaspoon salt
- ⅛ teaspoon black pepper
- ¼ cup olive oil
- ¼ cup vegetable oil

SALAD

- 8 cups packed baby spinach
- 1 cup diced tomatoes (about 2 medium)
- 1 cup drained mandarin oranges
- 1 cup glazed pecans*
- ½ cup crumbled feta cheese
- ½ cup diced red onion
- ½ cup dried cranberries
- 1 can (3 ounces) crispy rice noodles**
- 4 teaspoons toasted sesame seeds

Glazed pecans can be found in the produce section of many supermarkets (with other salad toppings). If unavailable, they can be prepared easily at home. (See Tip.)

**Crispy rice noodles can be found with canned chow mein noodles in the Asian section of the supermarket.*

1 For dressing, whisk vinegar, garlic, sugar, salt and pepper in medium bowl until blended. Slowly whisk in olive oil and vegetable oil until well blended.

2 For salad, divide spinach among four serving bowls. Top evenly with tomatoes, oranges, pecans, cheese, onion and cranberries. Sprinkle with rice noodles and sesame seeds. Drizzle each salad with 3 tablespoons dressing.

TIP

To make glazed pecans, combine 1 cup pecan halves, ¼ cup sugar, 1 tablespoon butter and ½ teaspoon salt in medium skillet; cook and stir over medium heat 5 minutes or until sugar mixture is dark brown and nuts are well coated. Spread on large plate; cool completely. Break into pieces or coarsely chop.

GARBAGE SALAD

MAKES 4 TO 6 SERVINGS

DRESSING

- ⅓ cup red wine vinegar
- 2 cloves garlic, minced
- 2 teaspoons sugar
- 1 teaspoon Italian seasoning
- ¼ teaspoon salt
- ¼ teaspoon black pepper
- ⅓ cup vegetable or canola oil

SALAD

- 1 package (5 ounces) spring mix
- 5 leaves romaine lettuce, chopped
- 1 small cucumber, diced
- 2 small plum tomatoes, diced
- ½ red onion, thinly sliced
- ¼ cup pitted kalamata olives
- 4 radishes, thinly sliced
- 4 ounces thinly sliced Genoa salami, cut into ¼-inch strips
- 4 ounces provolone cheese, cut into ¼-inch strips
- ¼ cup grated Parmesan cheese

1 For dressing, whisk vinegar, garlic, sugar, Italian seasoning, salt and pepper in small bowl until blended. Slowly whisk in oil until well blended.

2 Combine spring mix, romaine, cucumber, tomatoes, onion, olives and radishes in large bowl. Add half of dressing; toss gently to coat. Top with salami and provolone; sprinkle with Parmesan. Serve with remaining dressing.

AMAZING APPLE SALAD
MAKES 4 SERVINGS

DRESSING

- 5 tablespoons apple juice concentrate
- ¼ cup white balsamic vinegar
- 1 tablespoon lemon juice
- 1 tablespoon sugar
- ½ teaspoon salt
- ½ teaspoon onion powder
- ¼ teaspoon ground ginger
- 1 clove garlic, minced
- ¼ cup extra virgin olive oil

SALAD

- 12 cups mixed greens such as chopped romaine lettuce and spring greens
- 12 ounces thinly sliced cooked chicken
- 2 tomatoes, cut into wedges
- 1 package (about 3 ounces) dried apple chips
- ½ red onion, thinly sliced
- ½ cup crumbled Gorgonzola or blue cheese
- ½ cup pecans, toasted

1 For dressing, whisk apple juice concentrate, vinegar, lemon juice, sugar, salt, onion powder, ginger and garlic in small bowl until blended. Slowly whisk in oil until well blended.

2 For salad, divide greens among four serving bowls. Top with chicken, tomatoes, apple chips, onion, cheese and pecans.

3 Drizzle about 2 tablespoons dressing over each salad.

SALADS

SANDWICHES

BLT SUPREME
MAKES 2 SERVINGS

12 to 16 slices thick-cut bacon

⅓ cup mayonnaise

1½ teaspoons minced chipotle pepper in adobo sauce

1 teaspoon lime juice

1 ripe avocado

⅛ teaspoon salt

⅛ teaspoon black pepper

4 leaves romaine lettuce

½ baguette, cut into 2 (8-inch) lengths *or* 2 hoagie rolls, split and toasted

6 to 8 slices tomato

1 Cook bacon in skillet or oven until crisp-chewy. Drain on paper towel-lined plate.

2 Meanwhile, combine mayonnaise, chipotle pepper and lime juice in small bowl; mix well. Coarsely mash avocado in medium bowl; stir in salt and pepper. Cut romaine leaves crosswise into ¼-inch strips.

3 For each sandwich, spread heaping tablespoon mayonnaise mixture on bottom half of baguette; top with one fourth of lettuce. Arrange 3 to 4 slices bacon over lettuce; spread 2 tablespoons mashed avocado over bacon. Drizzle with heaping tablespoon mayonnaise mixture. Top with 3 to 4 tomato slices, one fourth of lettuce and 3 to 4 slices bacon. Close sandwich with top half of baguette.

CHICKEN AND ROASTED TOMATO PANINI

MAKES 4 SERVINGS

12 ounces plum tomatoes (about 2 large), cut into ⅛-inch slices

½ teaspoon coarse salt, divided

¼ teaspoon black pepper, divided

2 tablespoons olive oil, divided

4 boneless skinless chicken breasts (about 4 ounces each)

3 tablespoons butter, softened

¼ teaspoon garlic powder

¼ cup mayonnaise

2 tablespoons prepared pesto sauce

8 slices sourdough or rustic Italian bread

8 slices (about 1 ounce each) provolone cheese

½ cup baby spinach

1 Preheat oven to 400°F. Line baking sheet with parchment paper. Arrange tomato slices in single layer on prepared baking sheet. Sprinkle with ¼ teaspoon salt and ⅛ teaspoon pepper; drizzle with 1 tablespoon oil. Roast 20 to 25 minutes or until tomatoes are softened and begin to caramelize around edges.

2 Meanwhile, prepare chicken. If chicken breasts are thicker than ½ inch, pound to ½-inch thickness between sheets of plastic wrap. Heat remaining 1 tablespoon oil in large skillet over medium-high heat. Season both sides of chicken with remaining ¼ teaspoon salt and ⅛ teaspoon pepper. Add to skillet; cook about 6 minutes per side or until golden brown and cooked through. Remove to plate; let rest 10 minutes before slicing. Cut diagonally into ½-inch slices.

3 Combine butter and garlic powder in small bowl; mix well. Combine mayonnaise and pesto in another small bowl; mix well.

4 Spread one side of each bread slice with garlic butter. For each sandwich, place 1 slice bread, buttered side down, on plate. Spread with generous 1 tablespoon pesto mayonnaise. Layer with 1 provolone slice, 4 to 5 roasted tomato slices, 4 to 6 baby spinach leaves, 1 sliced chicken breast, second provolone slice and 4 to 6 baby spinach leaves. Top with second bread slice, buttered side up.

5 Preheat panini press, indoor grill or grill pan. Cook sandwiches until bread is golden brown and cheese is melted.

TUNA SALAD SANDWICH

MAKES 2 SERVINGS

1 can (12 ounces) solid white albacore tuna, drained

1 can (5 ounces) chunk white albacore tuna, drained

¼ cup mayonnaise

1 tablespoon pickle relish

2 teaspoons spicy brown mustard

1 teaspoon lemon juice

½ teaspoon salt

¼ teaspoon black pepper

2 pieces focaccia (about 4×3 inches), split and toasted *or* 4 slices honey wheat bread

Lettuce, tomato and red onion slices

1 Place tuna in medium bowl; flake with fork. Add mayonnaise, relish, mustard, lemon juice, salt and pepper; mix well.

2 Serve tuna salad on focaccia with lettuce, tomato and red onion.

CHICKEN FAJITA ROLL-UPS

MAKES 4 SERVINGS

1 cup ranch dressing

1 teaspoon chili powder

2 tablespoons vegetable oil, divided

2 teaspoons lime juice

2 teaspoons fajita seasoning

½ teaspoon chipotle chili powder

¼ teaspoon salt

4 boneless skinless chicken breasts (about 6 ounces each)

4 fajita-size flour tortillas (8 to 9 inches)

1 cup (4 ounces) shredded Cheddar cheese

1 cup (4 ounces) shredded Monterey Jack cheese

3 cups shredded lettuce

1 cup pico de gallo

1 Combine ranch dressing and 1 teaspoon chili powder in small bowl; mix well. Refrigerate until ready to serve.

2 Combine 1 tablespoon oil, lime juice, fajita seasoning, chipotle chili powder and salt in small bowl; mix well. Coat both sides of chicken with spice mixture.

3 Heat remaining 1 tablespoon oil in large nonstick skillet over medium-high heat. Add chicken in single layer; cook about 6 minutes per side or until no longer pink in center. Remove to plate; let rest 10 minutes before slicing. Cut chicken breasts in half lengthwise, then cut crosswise into ½-inch strips.

4 Wipe out skillet with paper towel. Place 1 tortilla in skillet; sprinkle ¼ cup Cheddar and ¼ cup Monterey Jack evenly over entire surface. Heat over medium heat until cheese is melted. Remove tortilla to clean work surface or cutting board.

5 Sprinkle ¾ cup shredded lettuce down center of 1 tortilla; top with ¼ cup pico de gallo and one fourth of chicken. Fold bottom of tortilla up over filling, then fold in sides and roll up. Cut in half diagonally. Repeat with remaining tortillas, cheese and fillings. Serve with ranch dipping sauce.

HEARTY VEGGIE SANDWICH

MAKES 4 SERVINGS

1 pound cremini mushrooms, stemmed and thinly sliced (⅛-inch slices)

2 tablespoons olive oil, divided

¾ teaspoon salt, divided

¼ teaspoon black pepper

1 medium zucchini, diced (¼-inch pieces, about 2 cups)

3 tablespoons butter, softened

8 slices artisan whole grain bread

¼ cup prepared pesto

¼ cup mayonnaise

2 cups packed baby spinach

4 slices (about 1 ounce each) mozzarella cheese

1 Preheat oven to 350°F. Combine mushrooms, 1 tablespoon oil, ½ teaspoon salt and pepper in medium bowl; toss to coat. Spread on large rimmed baking sheet. Roast 20 minutes or until mushrooms are dark brown and dry, stirring after 10 minutes. Cool on baking sheet.

2 Meanwhile, heat remaining 1 tablespoon oil in large skillet over medium heat. Add zucchini and remaining ¼ teaspoon salt; cook and stir 5 minutes or until zucchini is tender and lightly browned. Transfer to bowl; wipe out skillet with paper towels.

3 Spread butter over one side of each bread slice. Turn over slices. Spread pesto over 4 slices; spread mayonnaise over remaining 4 slices. Top pesto-covered slices evenly with mushrooms, then spinach, zucchini and cheese. Top with remaining bread slices, mayonnaise side down.

4 Heat same skillet over medium heat. Add sandwiches; cover and cook 2 minutes per side or until bread is toasted, spinach is slightly wilted and cheese is beginning to melt. Cut sandwiches in half; serve immediately.

SANDWICHES

BLACKENED CHICKEN TORTA

MAKES 4 SERVINGS

2 tablespoons vegetable oil

1½ tablespoons Creole seasoning

4 boneless skinless chicken breasts (6 to 8 ounces each)

½ cup sour cream

2 teaspoons lime juice, divided

½ teaspoon ground cumin

¼ teaspoon salt, divided

Dash black pepper

⅓ cup mayonnaise

½ teaspoon chipotle chili powder

1 ripe avocado

4 slices (about 1 ounce each) Cheddar cheese

4 slices (about 1 ounce each) pepper jack cheese

4 ciabatta or Kaiser rolls, split

1 cup finely shredded green cabbage or coleslaw mix

1 Combine oil and Creole seasoning in shallow dish; mix well. Add chicken; turn to coat thoroughly with spice mixture. Let stand while preparing sauces.

2 Combine sour cream, 1½ teaspoons lime juice, cumin, ⅛ teaspoon salt and dash of black pepper in medium bowl; mix well. Combine mayonnaise, chipotle chili powder, remaining ½ teaspoon lime juice and ⅛ teaspoon salt in small bowl; mix well. Mash avocado in another small bowl; season with additional salt and black pepper.

3 Heat cast iron skillet over medium-high heat until very hot. Add chicken to hot skillet; cook 6 minutes per side or until well browned and no longer pink in center. Remove to plate; top each chicken breast with 1 slice Cheddar and 1 slice pepper jack. Tent loosely with foil to melt cheese.

4 For each sandwich, spread 2 tablespoons sour cream mixture on bottom half of roll; top with mashed avocado, ¼ cup cabbage and cheese-topped chicken breast. Spread heaping tablespoon mayonnaise mixture on top half of roll; place over chicken.

TOMATO MOZZARELLA SANDWICH

MAKES 4 SERVINGS

BALSAMIC VINAIGRETTE

- 6 tablespoons extra virgin olive oil
- 3 tablespoons balsamic vinegar
- 1 clove garlic, minced
- 1 teaspoon honey
- 1 teaspoon Dijon mustard
- ½ teaspoon dried oregano
- ½ teaspoon salt
- ⅛ teaspoon black pepper

SANDWICHES

- 1 baguette, ends trimmed, cut into 4 equal pieces (4 ounces each) and split
- 1 cup loosely packed baby arugula
- 3 medium tomatoes, sliced ¼ inch thick
- 1 cup roasted red peppers, patted dry and thinly sliced
- 12 slices fresh mozzarella (one 8-ounce package)
- 12 fresh basil leaves

1 For vinaigrette, whisk oil, vinegar, garlic, honey, mustard, oregano, salt and pepper in small bowl until well blended.

2 For each sandwich, drizzle 1 tablespoon vinaigrette over bottom half of bread. Layer with arugula, tomato slices, roasted peppers, cheese slices, additional arugula and basil. Drizzle with 1 tablespoon dressing; replace top half of bread.

ALMOND CHICKEN SALAD SANDWICH

MAKES 4 SERVINGS

¼ cup mayonnaise

¼ cup plain Greek yogurt
  or sour cream

2 tablespoons cider vinegar

1 tablespoon honey

1 teaspoon salt

½ teaspoon black pepper

⅛ teaspoon garlic powder

2 cups chopped cooked chicken

¾ cup halved red grapes

1 large stalk celery, chopped

⅓ cup sliced almonds

  Leaf lettuce

1 tomato, thinly sliced

8 slices sesame semolina or
  country Italian bread

1 Whisk mayonnaise, yogurt, vinegar, honey, salt, pepper and garlic powder in small bowl until well blended.

2 Combine chicken, grapes and celery in medium bowl. Add dressing; toss gently to coat. Cover and refrigerate several hours or overnight. Stir in almonds just before making sandwiches.

3 Place lettuce and tomato slices on 4 bread slices; top with chicken salad and remaining bread slices. Serve immediately.

NEW ORLEANS-STYLE MUFFALETTA
MAKES 4 TO 6 SERVINGS

¾ cup pitted green olives

½ cup pitted kalamata olives

½ cup giardiniera (Italian-style pickled vegetables), drained

2 tablespoons fresh parsley leaves

2 tablespoons capers

1 clove garlic, minced

2 tablespoons olive oil

1 tablespoon red wine vinegar

1 (8-inch) round Italian or sesame seed loaf (16 to 22 ounces)

8 ounces thinly sliced ham

8 ounces thinly sliced Genoa salami

6 ounces thinly sliced provolone cheese

1 Combine olives, gardiniera, parsley, capers and garlic in food processor; pulse until coarsely chopped and no large pieces remain. Transfer to small bowl; stir in oil and vinegar until well blended. Cover and refrigerate several hours or overnight to blend flavors.

2 Cut bread in half crosswise. Spread two thirds of olive salad over bottom half of bread; layer with ham, salami and cheese. Spread remaining olive salad over cheese; top with top half of bread, pressing down slightly to compress. Wrap sandwich in plastic wrap; let stand 1 hour to blend flavors.

3 To serve sandwich warm, preheat oven to 350°F. Remove plastic wrap; wrap sandwich loosely in foil. Bake 5 to 10 minutes or just until sandwich is slightly warm and cheese begins to melt. Cut into wedges.

TURKEY ONION DIP

MAKES 6 SERVINGS

Herb-Roasted Turkey Breast
(recipe follows)

1 tablespoon olive oil

2 large onions, cut in half crosswise
then cut vertically into ¼-inch
slices (about 2 cups)

¼ cup water

½ teaspoon salt

1½ cups sour cream

⅓ cup prepared horseradish

3 tablespoons Dijon mustard

Black pepper

6 hoagie or sub rolls, split
and toasted

12 slices Swiss cheese
(about 1 ounce each)

1 Prepare Herb-Roasted Turkey Breast; let rest at least 15 minutes before shredding.

2 Meanwhile, heat oil in large skillet over medium-high heat. Add onions; cook
20 minutes or until onions begin to brown, stirring occasionally. Add water
and ½ teaspoon salt; cook over medium heat 20 minutes or until golden brown,
stirring occasionally.

3 Combine sour cream, horseradish and mustard in medium bowl; stir until well
blended. Refrigerate until ready to assemble sandwiches.

4 Shred turkey into bite-size pieces; place in large bowl. Drizzle with pan juices
and season with salt and pepper; toss to coat.

5 Spread cut sides of each roll with about 1½ tablespoons sour cream mixture. Top
bottom halves of rolls with 2 cups turkey, caramelized onions, 2 slices cheese
and top halves of rolls. Serve warm.

HERB-ROASTED TURKEY BREAST

MAKES ABOUT 6 SERVINGS

1 small bone-in turkey breast
(4 to 5 pounds)

1½ tablespoons olive oil

2 cloves garlic, minced

2 teaspoons coarse salt

1 teaspoon dried rosemary

1 teaspoon dried sage

½ teaspoon dried thyme

½ teaspoon black pepper

1 Preheat oven to 400°F. Place turkey breast on rack in small roasting or baking pan. Pat skin dry with paper towel.

2 Combine oil, garlic, salt, rosemary, sage, thyme and pepper in small bowl; mix well. Rub mixture all over turkey breast. (If desired, loosen skin and rub some of oil mixture directly on turkey meat.)

3 Place turkey in oven; *reduce oven temperature to 350°F.* Roast 1 hour 15 minutes or until cooked through (165°F). Let rest 15 minutes.

SANDWICHES

SPINACH VEGGIE WRAP

MAKES 4 SERVINGS

PICO DE GALLO

1 cup finely chopped tomatoes (about 2 small)

½ teaspoon salt

¼ cup chopped white onion

2 tablespoons minced jalapeño pepper

2 tablespoons chopped fresh cilantro

1 teaspoon lime juice

GUACAMOLE

2 large ripe avocados

¼ cup finely chopped red onion

2 tablespoons chopped fresh cilantro

2 teaspoons lime juice

½ teaspoon salt

WRAPS

4 whole wheat burrito-size tortillas (about 10 inches)

2 cups baby spinach

1 cup (about 4 ounces) sliced mushrooms

1 cup shredded Asiago cheese

Salsa

1 For pico de gallo, combine tomatoes and ½ teaspoon salt in fine-mesh strainer; set in bowl or sink to drain 15 minutes. Combine drained tomatoes, white onion, jalapeño, 2 tablespoons cilantro and 1 teaspoon lime juice in medium bowl; mix well.

2 For guacamole, combine avocados, red onion, 2 tablespoons cilantro, 2 teaspoons lime juice and ½ teaspoon salt in medium bowl; mash with fork to desired consistency.

3 For wraps, spread ¼ cup guacamole on each tortilla. Layer each with ½ cup spinach, ¼ cup mushrooms, ¼ cup cheese and ¼ cup pico de gallo. Roll up; serve with salsa.

MAIN DISHES

SPICY CHICKEN RIGATONI
MAKES 4 SERVINGS

2 tablespoons olive oil

2 cloves garlic, minced

½ teaspoon red pepper flakes

½ teaspoon black pepper

8 ounces boneless skinless chicken breasts, cut into thin strips

1 cup marinara sauce

¾ cup prepared Alfredo sauce

1 package (16 ounces) rigatoni or penne pasta, cooked until al dente

¾ cup frozen peas, thawed

Grated Parmesan cheese (optional)

1 Heat oil in large saucepan over medium-high heat. Add garlic, red pepper flakes and black pepper; cook and stir 1 minute. Add chicken; cook and stir 4 minutes or until cooked through.

2 Add marinara sauce and Alfredo sauce; stir until blended. Reduce heat to medium-low; cook 10 minutes, stirring occasionally.

3 Add pasta and peas; stir gently to coat. Cook 2 minutes or until heated through. Sprinkle with cheese, if desired.

PARMESAN-CRUSTED TILAPIA

MAKES 4 SERVINGS

⅔ cup plus 3 tablespoons grated Parmesan cheese, divided

⅔ cup panko bread crumbs

⅓ cup prepared Alfredo sauce (refrigerated or jarred)

1½ teaspoons dried parsley flakes

4 tilapia fillets (6 to 8 ounces each)

Shaved Parmesan cheese (optional)

Minced fresh parsley (optional)

1 Preheat oven to 425°F. Line baking sheet with foil; spray foil with nonstick cooking spray.

2 Combine ⅔ cup grated cheese and panko in medium bowl; mix well. Combine Alfredo sauce, remaining 3 tablespoons grated cheese and dried parsley in small bowl; mix well. Spread mixture over top of fish fillets, coating in thick even layer. Top with panko mixture, pressing in gently to adhere. Place fish on prepared baking sheet.

3 Bake on top shelf of oven about 15 minutes or until crust is golden brown and fish begins to flake when tested with fork. Garnish with shaved Parmesan and fresh parsley.

BANGKOK PEANUT NOODLES

MAKES 4 SERVINGS

SAUCE

- 6 tablespoons peanut butter
- ¼ cup soy sauce
- 1 tablespoon unseasoned rice vinegar
- 1 tablespoon packed brown sugar
- 1 tablespoon sriracha sauce
- 2 teaspoons grated fresh ginger
- 2 cloves garlic, minced
- 2 teaspoons dark sesame oil

STIR-FRY

- 1 package (6 ounces) dried chow mein stir-fry noodles
- 1 pound boneless skinless chicken breasts, cut into 1-inch pieces *or* 1 package (14 ounces) extra firm tofu, cut into ½-inch cubes
- ½ cup cornstarch
- 3 tablespoons vegetable oil, divided
- 1 red bell pepper, cut into thin strips
- ½ medium onion, thinly sliced
- 2 cups sliced Swiss chard or bok choy

1 For sauce, whisk peanut butter, soy sauce, vinegar, brown sugar, sriracha, ginger, garlic and sesame oil in small bowl until smooth.

2 For stir-fry, cook noodles according to package directions; drain and rinse under cold running water until cool.

3 Combine chicken and cornstarch in medium bowl; toss to coat. Heat 2 tablespoons vegetable oil in large skillet over medium-high heat. Add chicken; stir-fry 5 minutes or until golden brown and cooked through. Drain on paper towel-lined plate. Wipe out skillet with paper towel.

4 Heat remaining 1 tablespoon vegetable oil in same skillet over high heat. Add bell pepper and onion; stir-fry 5 minutes or until browned. Add chard; stir-fry 1 minute or until wilted. Add noodles and sauce; cook until noodles are coated with sauce. Add 1 tablespoon water if needed to loosen sauce. Return chicken to skillet; stir to coat. Cook just until heated through.

MAIN DISHES

CHICKEN MARSALA

MAKES 4 SERVINGS

4 boneless skinless chicken breasts
  (6 to 8 ounces each)

½ cup all-purpose flour

1 teaspoon coarse salt

¼ teaspoon black pepper

2 tablespoons olive oil

3 tablespoons butter, divided

2 cups (16 ounces) sliced
  mushrooms

1 shallot, minced (about
  2 tablespoons)

1 clove garlic, minced

1 cup dry Marsala wine

½ cup chicken broth

  Finely chopped fresh parsley

1 Pound chicken to ¼-inch thickness between two sheets of plastic wrap. Combine flour, salt and pepper in shallow dish; mix well. Coat both sides of chicken with flour mixture, shaking off excess.

2 Heat oil and 1 tablespoon butter in large skillet over medium-high heat. Add chicken in single layer; cook about 4 minutes per side or until golden brown. Remove to plate; cover loosely with foil to keep warm.

3 Add 1 tablespoon butter, mushrooms and shallot to skillet; cook about 10 minutes or until mushrooms are deep golden brown, stirring occasionally. Add garlic; cook and stir 1 minute. Add Marsala and broth; cook and stir 2 minutes, scraping up browned bits from bottom of skillet. Stir in remaining 1 tablespoon butter until melted.

4 Return chicken to skillet; turn to coat with sauce. Cook 2 minutes or until heated through. Sprinkle with parsley.

ISLAND FISH TACOS

MAKES 4 SERVINGS

COLESLAW

1 medium jicama (about 12 ounces), peeled and shredded

2 cups shredded coleslaw mix

3 tablespoons finely chopped fresh cilantro

¼ cup lime juice

¼ cup vegetable oil

3 tablespoons white vinegar

2 tablespoons mayonnaise

1 tablespoon honey

1 teaspoon salt

SALSA

2 medium tomatoes, diced (about 2 cups)

½ cup finely chopped red onion

¼ cup finely chopped fresh cilantro

2 tablespoons lime juice

2 tablespoons minced jalapeño pepper

1 teaspoon salt

TACOS

1 to 1¼ pounds white fish such as tilapia or mahi mahi, cut into 3×1½-inch pieces

Salt and black pepper

2 tablespoons vegetable oil

12 (6-inch) flour tortillas, heated

Guacamole (optional)

1 For coleslaw, combine jicama, coleslaw mix and 3 tablespoons cilantro in medium bowl. Whisk ¼ cup lime juice, ¼ cup oil, vinegar, mayonnaise, honey and 1 teaspoon salt in small bowl until well blended. Pour over vegetable mixture; stir to coat. Let stand at least 15 minutes for flavors to blend.

2 For salsa, place tomatoes in fine-mesh strainer; set in bowl or sink to drain 15 minutes. Transfer to another medium bowl. Stir in onion, ¼ cup cilantro, 2 tablespoons lime juice, jalapeño and 1 teaspoon salt; mix well.

3 For tacos, season both sides of fish with salt and black pepper. Heat 1 tablespoon oil in large nonstick skillet over medium-high heat. Add half of fish; cook about 2 minutes per side or until fish is opaque and begins to flake when tested with fork. Repeat with remaining oil and fish.

4 Serve fish in tortillas with coleslaw and salsa. Serve with guacamole, if desired.

VEGETABLE PENNE ITALIANO

MAKES 4 SERVINGS

1 tablespoon olive oil

1 red bell pepper, cut into
½-inch pieces

1 green bell pepper, cut into
½-inch pieces

1 medium sweet onion, halved
and thinly sliced

3 cloves garlic, minced

2 tablespoons tomato paste

2 teaspoons salt

1 teaspoon sugar

1 teaspoon Italian seasoning

¼ teaspoon black pepper

1 can (28 ounces) Italian plum
tomatoes, chopped, juice
reserved

8 ounces uncooked penne pasta

Grated Parmesan cheese

Chopped fresh basil

1 Heat oil in large skillet over medium-high heat. Add bell peppers, onion and garlic; cook and stir 8 minutes or until vegetables are crisp-tender.

2 Add tomato paste, salt, sugar, Italian seasoning and black pepper; cook and stir 1 minute. Stir in tomatoes with juice. Reduce heat to medium-low; cook 15 minutes or until vegetables are tender and sauce is thickened.

3 Meanwhile, cook pasta in large saucepan of boiling salted water according to package directions for al dente. Drain pasta; return to saucepan. Add sauce; stir gently to coat. Divide among four serving bowls; top with cheese and basil.

MEATBALLS AND RICOTTA
MAKES 5 TO 6 SERVINGS (20 MEATBALLS)

MEATBALLS

- 2 tablespoons olive oil
- ½ cup plain dry bread crumbs
- ½ cup milk
- 1 cup finely chopped yellow onion
- 2 green onions, finely chopped
- ½ cup grated Romano cheese, plus additional for serving
- 2 eggs, beaten
- ¼ cup finely chopped fresh parsley
- ¼ cup finely chopped fresh basil
- 2 cloves garlic, minced
- 2 teaspoons salt
- ¼ teaspoon black pepper
- 1 pound ground beef
- 1 pound ground pork

SAUCE

- 2 tablespoons olive oil
- 2 tablespoons butter
- 1 cup finely chopped yellow onion
- 1 clove garlic, minced
- 1 can (28 ounces) whole Italian plum tomatoes, coarsely chopped, juice reserved
- 1 can (28 ounces) crushed tomatoes
- 1 teaspoon salt
- ¼ teaspoon black pepper
- ¼ cup finely chopped fresh basil
- 1 to 1½ cups ricotta cheese

1 Preheat oven to 375°F. Brush 2 tablespoons oil over large rimmed baking sheet.

2 For meatballs, combine bread crumbs and milk in large bowl; mix well. Add 1 cup yellow onion, green onions, ½ cup Romano, eggs, parsley, ¼ cup basil, 2 cloves garlic, 2 teaspoons salt and ¼ teaspoon pepper; mix well. Add beef and pork; mix gently but thoroughly until blended. Shape mixture by ¼ cupfuls into balls. Place meatballs on prepared baking sheet; turn to coat with oil.

3 Bake about 20 minutes or until meatballs are cooked through (165°F).

4 Meanwhile, prepare sauce. Heat 2 tablespoons oil and butter in large saucepan over medium heat until butter is melted. Add 1 cup yellow onion; cook 8 minutes or until tender and lightly browned, stirring frequently. Add garlic; cook and stir 1 minute or until fragrant. Add plum tomatoes with juice, crushed tomatoes, 1 teaspoon salt and

¼ teaspoon pepper; bring to a simmer. Reduce heat to medium-low; cook 20 minutes, stirring occasionally.

5 Stir ¼ cup basil into sauce. Add meatballs; cook 10 minutes, stirring occasionally. Transfer meatballs and sauce to serving dish; dollop tablespoonfuls of ricotta between meatballs. Garnish with additional Romano.

MAIN DISHES

PESTO CAVATAPPI

MAKES 4 TO 6 SERVINGS

PESTO

- 2 cups packed fresh basil leaves*
- 1 cup walnuts, toasted
- ½ cup shredded Parmesan cheese, plus additional for garnish
- 4 cloves garlic
- 1 teaspoon salt
- ¼ teaspoon black pepper
- ¾ cup extra virgin olive oil

PASTA

- 1 package (16 ounces) uncooked cavatappi pasta
- 1 tablespoon extra virgin olive oil
- 2 plum tomatoes, diced (1½ cups)
- 1 package (8 ounces) sliced mushrooms
- ¼ cup dry white wine
- ¼ cup vegetable broth
- ¼ cup whipping cream

Or substitute 1 cup packed fresh parsley leaves for half of basil.

1 For pesto, combine basil, walnuts, ½ cup cheese, garlic, salt and pepper in food processor; pulse until coarsely chopped. With motor running, slowly add ¾ cup oil in thin steady stream; process until well blended. Measure 1 cup pesto for pasta; reserve remaining pesto for another use.

2 Cook pasta in large saucepan of boiling salted water according to package directions for al dente. Drain pasta; return to saucepan.

3 Meanwhile, heat 1 tablespoon olive oil in large skillet over medium-high heat. Add tomatoes and mushrooms; cook about 7 minutes or until most of liquid has evaporated, stirring occasionally. Add wine, broth and cream; bring to a boil. Reduce heat to low; cook about 4 minutes or until sauce has thickened slightly. Stir in 1 cup pesto; cook just until heated through.

4 Pour sauce over pasta; stir gently to coat. Divide pasta among serving bowls; garnish with additional cheese.

BOURBON-MARINATED SALMON

MAKES 4 SERVINGS

¼ cup packed brown sugar

¼ cup bourbon

¼ cup soy sauce

2 tablespoons lime juice

1 tablespoon grated fresh ginger

1 tablespoon minced garlic

¼ teaspoon black pepper

4 salmon fillets (7 to 8 ounces each)

2 tablespoons finely chopped green onion

1 Combine brown sugar, bourbon, soy sauce, lime juice, ginger, garlic and pepper in medium bowl; mix well. Reserve ¼ cup mixture for serving; set aside.

2 Place salmon in large resealable food storage bag. Pour remaining bourbon mixture over salmon; seal bag and turn to coat. Marinate in refrigerator 2 to 4 hours, turning occasionally.

3 Prepare grill or preheat broiler. Remove salmon from marinade; discard marinade.

4 Grill or broil salmon 10 minutes or until fish begins to flake when tested with fork. (To broil, place salmon on foil-lined baking sheet sprayed with nonstick cooking spray.) Brush with reserved marinade mixture; sprinkle with green onion.

CLASSIC LASAGNA

MAKES 6 TO 8 SERVINGS

1 tablespoon olive oil

8 ounces bulk mild Italian sausage

8 ounces ground beef

1 medium onion, chopped

3 cloves garlic, minced, divided

1½ teaspoons salt, divided

1 can (28 ounces) crushed tomatoes

1 can (28 ounces) diced tomatoes

2 teaspoons Italian seasoning

1 egg

1 container (15 ounces) ricotta cheese

¾ cup grated Parmesan cheese, divided

½ cup minced fresh parsley

¼ teaspoon black pepper

12 uncooked no-boil lasagna noodles

4 cups (16 ounces) shredded mozzarella

1 Preheat oven to 350°F. Spray 13×9-inch baking dish with nonstick cooking spray.

2 Heat oil in large saucepan over medium-high heat. Add sausage, beef, onion, 2 cloves garlic and 1 teaspoon salt; cook and stir 10 minutes or until meat is no longer pink, breaking up meat with wooden spoon. Add crushed tomatoes, diced tomatoes and Italian seasoning; bring to a boil. Reduce heat to medium-low; cook 15 minutes, stirring occasionally.

3 Meanwhile, beat egg in medium bowl. Stir in ricotta, ½ cup Parmesan, parsley, remaining 1 clove garlic, ½ teaspoon salt and pepper until well blended.

4 Spread ¼ cup sauce in prepared baking dish. Top with 3 noodles, breaking to fit if necessary. Spread one third of ricotta mixture over noodles. Sprinkle with 1 cup mozzarella; top with 2 cups sauce. Repeat layers of noodles, ricotta mixture, mozzarella and sauce two times. Top with remaining 3 noodles, sauce, 1 cup mozzarella and ¼ cup Parmesan. Cover dish with foil sprayed with cooking spray.

5 Bake 30 minutes. Remove foil; bake 10 to 15 minutes or until hot and bubbly. Let stand 10 minutes before serving.

DUTCH BABY PANCAKE

MAKES 2 SERVINGS

3 tablespoons butter, divided, plus additional for serving

½ cup all-purpose flour

2 tablespoons granulated sugar

¼ teaspoon salt

½ cup whole milk, at room temperature

2 eggs, at room temperature

¼ teaspoon vanilla

Powdered sugar

Lemon wedges

1 Preheat oven to 400°F. Place 1 tablespoon butter in 9- to 10-inch ovenproof skillet; place skillet in oven to heat while preparing batter. Melt remaining 2 tablespoons butter; let cool slightly.

2 Combine flour, granulated sugar and salt in medium bowl; mix well. Add milk, eggs, melted butter and vanilla; whisk 1 minute or until batter is very smooth.

3 Remove skillet from oven; immediately pour batter into hot skillet.

4 Bake about 20 minutes or until outside of pancake is puffed and edges are deep golden brown. Sprinkle with powdered sugar; serve with lemon wedges and additional butter.

PASTA CAMPAGNOLO

MAKES 4 SERVINGS

3 tablespoons olive oil

8 ounces Italian sausage, casings removed

1 small onion, finely chopped

1 red bell pepper, cut into ¼-inch strips

2 cloves garlic, minced

⅓ cup dry white wine

1 can (28 ounces) crushed tomatoes

1 can (8 ounces) tomato sauce

4 tablespoons chopped fresh basil, divided, plus addtional for garnish

½ teaspoon salt

¼ teaspoon black pepper

⅛ teaspoon red pepper flakes

1 package (16 ounces) uncooked rigatoni or penne pasta

¼ cup grated Romano cheese

1 package (4 ounces) goat cheese, cut crosswise into 8 slices

1 Heat oil in large saucepan over medium heat. Break sausage into small (½-inch) pieces; add to saucepan. Cook about 5 minutes or until browned, stirring occasionally. Add onion and bell pepper; cook and stir 4 minutes or until vegetables are softened. Add garlic; cook and stir 1 minute.

2 Add wine; cook about 5 minutes or until most of liquid has evaporated. Stir in tomatoes, tomato sauce, 2 tablespoons basil, salt, black pepper and red pepper flakes; bring to a boil. Reduce heat to medium-low; cook 20 minutes or until sauce has thickened slightly.

3 Meanwhile, cook pasta in large saucepan of boiling salted water according to package directions for al dente. Add hot cooked pasta, Romano and remaining 2 tablespoons basil to sauce; stir gently to coat. Cook until heated through.

4 Top with goat cheese; garnish with additional basil.

SPINACH ARTICHOKE EGG SOUFFLÉS

MAKES 8 SERVINGS

1 package frozen puff pastry (2 sheets), thawed according to package directions

1 teaspoon olive oil

¼ cup chopped onion

1 clove garlic, minced

¼ cup finely chopped roasted red pepper (1 pepper)

¼ cup finely chopped canned artichoke hearts (about 2 medium)

¼ cup thawed frozen spinach, squeezed dry

3 eggs, separated

½ (8-ounce) package cream cheese, softened

½ teaspoon salt

⅛ teaspoon black pepper

4 tablespoons grated Romano cheese, divided

1 Preheat oven to 400°F. Spray eight 4-inch or 1-cup ramekins or jumbo (3½-inch) muffin pan cups with nonstick cooking spray. Unfold puff pastry; cut each sheet into quarters. Gently press each pastry square into bottoms and partially up sides of prepared ramekins. (Pastry should not reach tops of ramekins.) Place ramekins on baking sheet; refrigerate while preparing filling.

2 Heat oil in medium skillet over medium heat. Add onion; cook and stir 2 minutes or until softened and lightly browned. Add garlic; cook and stir 30 seconds. Add roasted pepper, artichokes and spinach; cook and stir 2 minutes or until all liquid has evaporated.

3 Whisk egg yolks, cream cheese, salt and pepper in medium bowl until well blended. Stir in vegetable mixture and 3 tablespoons Romano.

4 Beat egg whites in large bowl with electric mixer at high speed 3 minutes or until stiff peaks form. Fold into vegetable mixture until blended. Divide mixture evenly among pastry-lined ramekins; sprinkle with remaining 1 tablespoon Romano. Fold points of pastry in towards center.

5 Bake 25 minutes or until pastry is golden brown and filling is puffed. Cool in ramekins 2 minutes; remove to wire rack. Serve warm.

BRUSCHETTA CHICKEN FETTUCCINE

MAKES 4 SERVINGS

BALSAMIC GLAZE

- ¼ cup balsamic vinegar
- 2 tablespoons packed brown sugar
- 1 teaspoon molasses
- ¼ teaspoon salt

BRUSCHETTA SAUCE

- 4 cups diced plum tomatoes (about 4 medium)
- ½ cup tomato sauce
- ¼ cup olive oil
- ¼ cup chopped fresh basil
- 1 tablespoon white wine vinegar
- 2 cloves garlic, minced
- ¾ teaspoon salt
- ½ teaspoon black pepper

CHICKEN AND PASTA

- 4 boneless skinless chicken breasts (4 ounces each)
- Salt and black pepper
- ¼ teaspoon garlic powder
- 1 tablespoon olive oil
- 1 package (16 ounces) uncooked fettuccine
- ¼ cup grated Parmesan cheese
- Shaved Parmesan cheese (optional)
- Chopped fresh parsley (optional)

1 For glaze, combine balsamic vinegar, brown sugar, molasses and ¼ teaspoon salt in small saucepan; bring to a simmer over medium heat. Cook about 10 minutes or until reduced by half. Set aside to cool.

2 For sauce, combine tomatoes, tomato sauce, ¼ cup oil, basil, white wine vinegar, garlic, ¾ teaspoon salt and ½ teaspoon pepper in medium bowl; mix well.

3 If necessary, pound chicken to ¾-inch thickness between two sheets of plastic wrap. Season with salt, pepper and garlic powder. Heat 1 tablespoon oil in large skillet over medium-high heat. Add chicken; cook about 6 minutes per side or until golden brown and no longer pink in center. Remove to plate; cover loosely to keep warm.

4 Meanwhile, cook fettuccine in large saucepan of boiling salted water according to package directions for al dente. Drain in colander; return empty saucepan to stove. Add sauce mixture to saucepan; cook and stir over high heat 2 minutes or until heated through. Add fettuccine and ¼ cup grated Parmesan to saucepan; toss to coat.

5 Slice chicken. Divide pasta among four serving bowls; drizzle with glaze. Top each serving with sliced chicken breast; garnish with shaved Parmesan and parsley. Serve immediately.

MAIN DISHES

RESTAURANT-STYLE BABY BACK RIBS

MAKES 4 SERVINGS

1¼ cups water

1 cup white vinegar

⅔ cup packed dark brown sugar

½ cup tomato paste

1 tablespoon yellow mustard

1½ teaspoons salt

1 teaspoon liquid smoke

1 teaspoon onion powder

½ teaspoon garlic powder

½ teaspoon paprika

2 racks pork baby back ribs
(3½ to 4 pounds total)

1 Combine water, vinegar, brown sugar, tomato paste, mustard, salt, liquid smoke, onion powder, garlic powder and paprika in medium saucepan; bring to a boil over medium heat. Reduce heat to medium-low; cook 40 minutes or until sauce thickens, stirring occasionally.

2 Preheat oven to 300°F. Place each rack of ribs on large sheet of heavy-duty foil. Brush some of sauce over ribs, covering completely. Fold down edges of foil tightly to seal and create packet. Place foil packets on baking sheet, seam sides up.

3 Bake 2 hours. Prepare grill or preheat broiler. Carefully remove ribs from foil; drain off excess liquid.

4 Brush ribs with sauce; grill or broil about 5 minutes per side or until beginning to char, brushing with sauce again during grilling. Serve with remaining sauce.

EGGPLANT PARMESAN

MAKES 4 SERVINGS

2 tablespoons olive oil

2 cloves garlic, minced

1 can (28 ounces) Italian whole tomatoes, undrained

½ cup water

1¼ teaspoons salt, divided

¼ teaspoon dried oregano

Pinch red pepper flakes

1 eggplant (about 1 pound)

⅓ cup all-purpose flour

Black pepper

⅔ cup milk

1 egg

1 cup Italian-seasoned dry bread crumbs

4 to 5 tablespoons vegetable oil, divided

1 cup (4 ounces) shredded mozzarella cheese

Chopped fresh parsley

1 Heat olive oil in medium saucepan over medium heat. Add garlic; cook and stir 2 minutes or until softened (do not brown). Crush tomatoes with hands (in bowl or in can); add to saucepan with juices from can. Stir in water, 1 teaspoon salt, oregano and red pepper flakes; bring to a simmer. Reduce heat to medium-low; cook 45 minutes, stirring occasionally.

2 Meanwhile, prepare eggplant. Cut eggplant crosswise into ¼-inch slices. Combine flour, remaining ¼ teaspoon salt and black pepper in shallow dish. Beat milk and egg in another shallow dish. Place bread crumbs in third shallow dish.

3 Coat both sides of eggplant slices with flour mixture, shaking off excess. Dip in egg mixture, letting excess drip back into dish. Roll in bread crumbs to coat. Place in single layer on baking sheet. Preheat broiler.

4 Heat 3 tablespoons vegetable oil in large skillet over medium-high heat. Working in batches, add eggplant slices to skillet in single layer; cook 3 to 4 minutes per side or until golden brown, adding additional vegetable oil as needed. Remove to paper towel-lined plate; cover loosely with foil to keep warm.

5 Spray 13×9-inch baking dish with nonstick cooking spray. Arrange eggplant slices overlapping in baking dish; top with half of warm marinara sauce. (Reserve remaining marinara sauce for pasta or another use.) Sprinkle with cheese.

6 Broil 2 to 3 minutes or just until cheese is melted and beginning to brown. Garnish with parsley.

MAIN DISHES

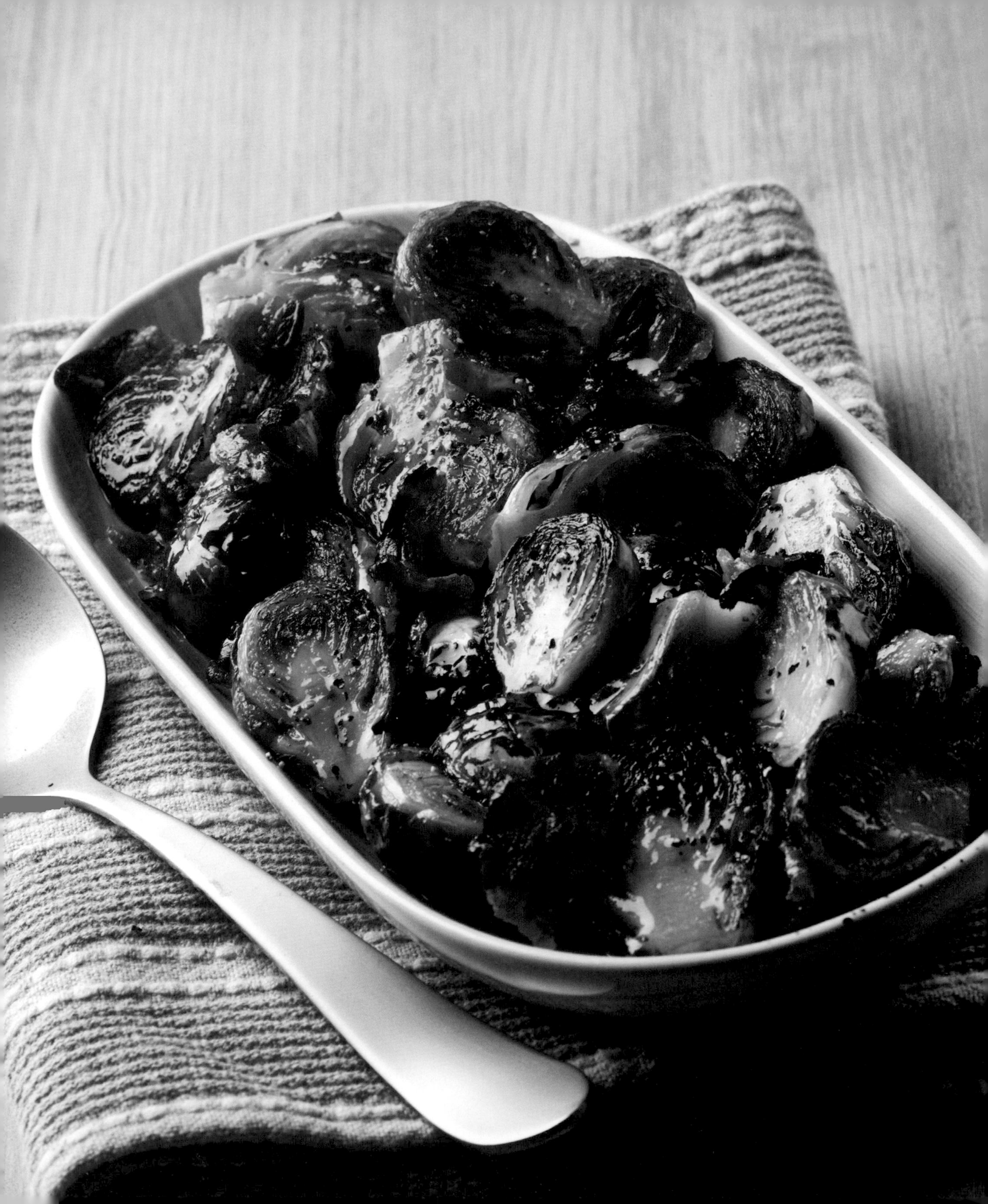

SIDE DISHES

BRUSSELS SPROUTS WITH HONEY BUTTER

MAKES 4 SERVINGS

6 slices thick-cut bacon, cut into ½-inch pieces

1½ pounds brussels sprouts (about 24 medium), halved

¼ teaspoon salt

¼ teaspoon black pepper

2 tablespoons butter, softened

2 tablespoons honey

1 Preheat oven to 375°F. Cook bacon in medium skillet until almost crisp. Drain on paper towel-lined plate; set aside. Reserve 1 tablespoon drippings for cooking brussels sprouts.

2 Place brussels sprouts on large baking sheet. Drizzle with reserved bacon drippings and sprinkle with ¼ teaspoon salt and ¼ teaspoon pepper; toss to coat. Spread in single layer on baking sheet.

3 Roast 30 minutes or until brussels sprouts are browned, stirring once.

4 Combine butter and honey in medium bowl; mix well. Add roasted brussels sprouts; stir until completely coated. Stir in bacon; season with additional salt and pepper.

CHICKEN FRIED RICE

MAKES 4 SERVINGS

2 tablespoons vegetable oil, divided

12 ounces boneless skinless chicken breasts, cut into ½-inch pieces

Salt and black pepper

2 tablespoons butter

2 cloves garlic, minced

½ sweet onion, diced

1 medium carrot, diced

2 green onions, thinly sliced

3 eggs

4 cups cooked white rice*

3 tablespoons soy sauce

2 tablespoons sesame seeds

*For 4 cups cooked rice, prepare 1½ cups white rice according to package directions without oil or butter. Spread hot rice on large rimmed baking sheet; cool to room temperature. Refrigerate several hours or overnight. Measure 4 cups for recipe.

1 Heat 1 tablespoon oil in large skillet over medium-high heat. Add chicken; season with salt and pepper. Stir-fry 5 to 6 minutes or until cooked through. Add butter and garlic; cook and stir 1 minute or until butter is melted. Remove to medium bowl.

2 Add sweet onion, carrot and green onions to skillet; cook and stir over high heat 3 minutes or until vegetables are softened. Add to bowl with chicken.

3 Heat remaining 1 tablespoon oil in same skillet. Crack eggs into skillet; cook and stir 45 seconds or until eggs are scrambled but still moist. Add chicken and vegetable mixture, rice, soy sauce and sesame seeds; cook and stir 2 minutes or until well blended and heated through. Season with additional salt and pepper.

BROCCOLI AND CHEESE

MAKES 4 TO 6 SERVINGS

2 medium crowns broccoli (1½ pounds), cut into florets (about 6½ cups)

2 tablespoons butter

2 tablespoons all-purpose flour

1½ cups milk

½ teaspoon salt

⅛ teaspoon ground nutmeg

⅛ teaspoon ground red pepper

1 cup (4 ounces) shredded Cheddar cheese

½ cup (2 ounces) shredded Monterey Jack cheese

¼ cup shredded Parmesan cheese

Paprika (optional)

1 Bring large saucepan of water to a boil over medium-high heat. Add broccoli; cook 7 minutes or until tender.

2 Meanwhile, melt butter in medium saucepan over medium-high heat. Add flour; whisk until smooth. Gradually whisk in milk until well blended. Cook 2 minutes or until thickened, whisking frequently. Stir in salt, nutmeg and red pepper. Reduce heat to low; whisk in cheeses in three additions, whisking well after first two additions and stirring just until blended after last addition.

3 Drain broccoli; place on serving plates. Top with cheese sauce; garnish with paprika. Serve immediately.

GARLIC KNOTS
MAKES 20 KNOTS

¾ cup warm water (105° to 115°F)

1 package (¼ ounce) active dry yeast

1 teaspoon sugar

2¼ cups all-purpose flour

2 tablespoons olive oil, divided

1½ teaspoons salt, divided

4 tablespoons (½ stick) butter, divided

1 tablespoon minced garlic

¼ teaspoon garlic powder

½ cup grated Parmesan cheese

2 tablespoons chopped fresh parsley

½ teaspoon dried oregano

1 Combine water, yeast and sugar in large bowl of electric stand mixer; stir to dissolve yeast. Let stand 5 minutes or until bubbly. Stir in flour, 1 tablespoon oil and 1 teaspoon salt; knead with dough hook at low speed 5 minutes or until dough is smooth and elastic. Shape dough into a ball. Place in large greased bowl; turn to grease top. Cover and let rise in warm place 1 hour or until doubled in size.

2 Melt 2 tablespoons butter in small saucepan over low heat. Add remaining 1 tablespoon oil, ½ teaspoon salt, garlic and garlic powder; cook over very low heat 5 minutes. Pour into small bowl; set aside.

3 Preheat oven to 400°F. Line baking sheet with parchment paper.

4 Turn out dough onto lightly floured surface. Punch down dough; let stand 10 minutes. Roll out dough into 10×8-inch rectangle. Cut into 20 (2-inch) squares. Roll each piece into 8-inch rope; tie in a knot. Brush knots with garlic mixture; place on prepared baking sheet.

5 Bake 10 minutes or until knots are lightly browned. Meanwhile, melt remaining 2 tablespoons butter. Combine cheese, parsley and oregano in small bowl; mix well. Brush melted butter over baked knots; immediately sprinkle with cheese mixture. Cool slightly on baking sheet. Serve warm.

CINNAMON APPLES

MAKES 4 SERVINGS

¼ cup (½ stick) butter

3 tart red apples such as Fuji, Braeburn or Honeycrisp (about 1½ pounds total), peeled and cut into ½-inch wedges

¼ cup packed brown sugar

1 teaspoon ground cinnamon

⅛ teaspoon ground nutmeg

⅛ teaspoon salt

1 tablespoon cornstarch

1 Melt butter in large skillet over medium-high heat. Add apples; cook about 8 minutes or until apples are tender, stirring occasionally.

2 Add brown sugar, cinnamon, nutmeg and salt; cook and stir 1 minute or until glazed. Reduce heat to medium-low; stir in cornstarch until well blended.

3 Remove from heat; let stand 5 minutes for glaze to thicken. Stir again; serve immediately.

GREEN BEANS WITH GARLIC-CILANTRO BUTTER

MAKES 4 TO 6 SERVINGS

1½ pounds green beans, ends trimmed

3 tablespoons butter

1 red bell pepper, cut into thin strips

½ sweet onion, halved and thinly sliced

2 teaspoons minced garlic

1 teaspoon salt

2 tablespoons chopped fresh cilantro

Black pepper

1 Bring large saucepan of salted water to a boil over medium-high heat. Add beans; cook 6 minutes or until tender. Drain beans; return to saucepan.

2 Meanwhile, melt butter in large skillet over medium-high heat. Add bell pepper and onion; cook and stir 3 minutes or until vegetables are tender but not browned. Add garlic; cook and stir 30 seconds.

3 Add beans and salt; cook and stir 2 minutes or until heated through and beans are coated with butter. Stir in cilantro; season with black pepper. Serve immediately.

HEARTY HASH BROWN CASSEROLE

MAKES ABOUT 16 SERVINGS

2 cups sour cream

2 cups (8 ounces) shredded
Colby cheese, divided

1 can (10¾ ounces) cream of
chicken soup

½ cup (1 stick) butter, melted

1 small onion, finely chopped

¾ teaspoon salt

½ teaspoon black pepper

1 package (30 ounces) frozen
shredded hash brown
potatoes, thawed

1 Preheat oven to 375°F. Spray 13×9-inch baking dish with nonstick cooking spray.

2 Combine sour cream, 1½ cups cheese, soup, butter, onion, salt and pepper in large bowl; mix well. Add potatoes; stir until well blended. Spread mixture in prepared baking dish. (Do not pack down.) Sprinkle with remaining ½ cup cheese.

3 Bake about 45 minutes or until cheese is melted and top of casserole is beginning to brown.

CAJUN RICE

MAKES 8 TO 10 SERVINGS

2 cups uncooked long grain rice

4 cups water, divided

1¼ teaspoons salt, divided

4 green onions, finely chopped, green and white parts separated

8 ounces ground beef

8 ounces chicken gizzards,* minced

½ cup finely chopped green bell pepper

1 teaspoon Cajun or Creole seasoning

½ teaspoon garlic powder

¼ teaspoon celery seed

¼ teaspoon ground red pepper

¼ teaspoon black pepper

Or substitute an additional 8 ounces ground beef for the chicken gizzards.

1 Rinse rice in strainer under cold running water; drain. Combine rice, 3¾ cups water and 1 teaspoon salt in medium saucepan; bring to a boil over medium-high heat. Reduce heat to low; cover and cook about 17 minutes or until liquid is absorbed and rice is tender but still firm. Remove from heat; let stand, covered, 5 minutes. Fluff rice with fork; stir in green parts of green onions.

2 Meanwhile, cook beef in large deep skillet over medium-high heat 5 minutes until beef is no longer pink, stirring frequently. Remove to plate; drain fat. Add chicken gizzards and bell pepper to skillet; cook 7 minutes or until chicken is cooked through. Add white parts of green onions, Cajun seasoning, garlic powder, celery seed, red pepper, black pepper and remaining ¼ teaspoon salt; cook and stir 2 minutes. Return beef to skillet; mix well.

3 Stir in rice and remaining ¼ cup water; cook over medium-low heat 15 minutes, stirring occasionally.

LOADED BAKED POTATOES

MAKES 4 SERVINGS

4 large baking potatoes

1 cup (4 ounces) shredded Cheddar cheese

1 cup (4 ounces) shredded Monterey Jack cheese

8 slices bacon, crisp-cooked

½ cup sour cream

¼ cup (½ stick) butter, melted

2 tablespoons milk

1 teaspoon salt

¼ teaspoon black pepper

1 tablespoon vegetable oil

2 teaspoons coarse sea salt

1 green onion, thinly sliced

1 Preheat oven to 400°F. Poke potatoes all over with fork; place in small baking pan. Bake about 1 hour or until potatoes are fork-tender. Let stand until cool enough to handle. *Reduce oven temperature to 350°F.*

2 Combine Cheddar and Monterey Jack in small bowl; reserve ¼ cup for garnish. Chop bacon; reserve ¼ cup for garnish.

3 Cut off thin slice from one long side of each potato. Scoop out centers of potatoes, leaving ¼-inch shell. Place flesh from 3 potatoes in medium bowl. (Reserve flesh from fourth potato for another use.) Add sour cream, butter, remaining 1¾ cups shredded cheese, bacon, milk, 1 teaspoon salt and pepper to bowl with potatoes; mash until well blended.

4 Turn potato shells over; brush bottoms and sides with oil. Sprinkle evenly with sea salt. Turn right side up and return to baking pan. Fill shells with mashed potato mixture, mounding over tops of shells. Sprinkle with reserved cheese and bacon.

5 Bake about 20 minutes or until filling is hot and cheese is melted. Sprinkle with green onion.

TRUFFLE MACARONI AND CHEESE
MAKES 6 TO 8 SERVINGS

1 pound uncooked ditalini pasta

½ cup (1 stick) butter, divided

¼ cup all-purpose flour

4 cups whole milk

1 teaspoon salt

¼ teaspoon ground nutmeg

8 ounces smoked mozzarella, shredded

5 ounces fontina cheese, shredded

5 ounces Asiago cheese, shredded

4 ounces Cheddar cheese, shredded

½ cup grated Romano cheese

2 tablespoons truffle oil

1 clove garlic, minced

¼ teaspoon Italian seasoning

4 cups cubed French bread (½-inch cubes)

1 Preheat oven to 375°F. Cook pasta in large saucepan of boiling salted water 9 minutes or until al dente. Drain and set aside.

2 Melt ¼ cup butter in large saucepan over medium heat. Add flour; whisk until smooth and well blended. Slowly whisk in milk in thin steady stream. Add salt and nutmeg; cook about 7 minutes or until thickened, whisking frequently.

3 Combine mozzarella, fontina, Asiago and Cheddar in large bowl; reserve 1½ cups for topping. Gradually add remaining cheese mixture by handfuls to milk mixture, whisking until smooth after each addition. Stir in Romano until blended. Stir in truffle oil. Add cooked pasta; stir until well blended. Spread in 2-quart baking dish or individual baking dishes; top with reserved cheeses.

4 Melt remaining ¼ cup butter in large skillet over medium-high heat. Add garlic and Italian seasoning; cook and stir 30 seconds or until garlic is fragrant but not browned. Add bread cubes; stir to coat. Spread over top of pasta.

5 Bake about 20 minutes or until cheese is bubbly and bread cubes are golden brown.

STEAKHOUSE CREAMED SPINACH

MAKES 4 SERVINGS

1 pound baby spinach

½ cup (1 stick) butter

2 tablespoons finely chopped onion

¼ cup all-purpose flour

2 cups whole milk

1 bay leaf

½ teaspoon salt

Pinch ground nutmeg

Pinch ground red pepper

Black pepper

1 Heat medium saucepan of water to a boil over high heat. Add spinach; cook 1 minute. Drain and transfer to bowl of ice water to stop cooking. Drain and squeeze spinach dry; coarsely chop. Wipe out saucepan with paper towel.

2 Melt butter in same saucepan over medium heat. Add onion; cook and stir 2 minutes or until softened. Add flour; cook and stir 2 to 3 minutes or until slightly golden. Slowly add milk in thin steady stream, whisking constantly until mixture boils and begins to thicken. Stir in bay leaf, ½ teaspoon salt, nutmeg and red pepper. Reduce heat to low; cook 5 minutes, stirring frequently. Remove and discard bay leaf.

3 Stir in spinach; cook 5 minutes, stirring frequently. Season with additional salt and black pepper.

JALAPEÑO BEANS

MAKES 4 TO 6 SERVINGS

1 tablespoon vegetable oil

1 small onion, finely chopped

1 teaspoon ground cumin

1 teaspoon garlic powder

½ teaspoon smoked paprika

¼ teaspoon ground red pepper

3 tablespoons chopped pickled jalapeño peppers

2 cans (about 15 ounces each) chili beans (made with pinto beans)

⅓ cup dark lager beer

1 tablespoon white vinegar

1 teaspoon sugar

½ teaspoon hot pepper sauce

Salt and black pepper

1 Heat oil in medium saucepan over medium-high heat. Add onion; cook and stir 2 minutes or until translucent. Add cumin, garlic powder, paprika and red pepper; cook and stir 1 minute. Add pickled jalapeños; cook and stir 30 seconds.

2 Stir in beans, beer, vinegar, sugar and hot pepper sauce; bring to a boil. Reduce heat to medium-low; cook 15 minutes, stirring occasionally. Season with salt and black pepper. Beans will thicken upon standing.

CHEESY SPINACH CASSEROLE

MAKES 6 TO 8 SERVINGS

1 pound baby spinach

4 slices bacon, chopped

1 small onion, chopped

1 cup (4 ounces) sliced mushrooms

¼ cup chopped red bell pepper

3 cloves garlic, minced

1½ teaspoons minced chipotle pepper in adobo sauce

1 teaspoon seasoned salt

8 ounces pasteurized process cheese product, cut into pieces

½ (8-ounce) package cream cheese, cut into pieces

1 cup thawed frozen corn

½ cup (2 ounces) shredded Monterey Jack and Cheddar cheese blend

1 Preheat oven to 350°F. Spray 1-quart baking dish with nonstick cooking spray.

2 Heat large saucepan of water to a boil over high heat. Add spinach; cook 1 minute. Drain and transfer to bowl of ice water to stop cooking. Drain and squeeze spinach dry; set aside. Wipe out saucepan with paper towel.

3 Cook bacon in same saucepan over medium-high heat until almost crisp, stirring frequently. Drain off all but 1 tablespoon drippings. Add onion to saucepan; cook and stir 3 minutes or until softened. Add mushrooms and bell pepper; cook and stir 5 minutes or until vegetables are tender. Add garlic, chipotle pepper and seasoned salt; cook and stir 1 minute.

4 Add process cheese and cream cheese to saucepan; cook until melted, stirring frequently. Add spinach and corn; cook and stir 3 minutes. Transfer to prepared baking dish; sprinkle with shredded cheese blend.

5 Bake 20 to 25 minutes or until cheese is melted and casserole is bubbly. If desired, broil 1 to 2 minutes to brown top of casserole.

DESSERTS

ICE CREAM PIZZA TREAT
MAKES 8 SERVINGS

24 chocolate sandwich cookies

1 jar (about 12 ounces) hot fudge topping, divided

2 pints vanilla ice cream

⅓ cup candy-coated chocolate pieces

1 Place cookies in food processor; pulse until large crumbs form. (Do not overprocess into fine crumbs.) Add ½ cup fudge topping; pulse just until blended. (Mixture should not be smooth; small cookie pieces may remain.)

2 Transfer mixture to pizza pan; press into 11- to 12-inch circle about ¼ inch thick. Freeze crust 10 minutes. Meanwhile, remove ice cream from freezer to soften 10 minutes.

3 Spread ice cream evenly over crust about ½ inch thick, leaving ½-inch border around edges. Return to freezer; freeze 2 hours or until firm.

4 Heat remaining fudge topping according to package directions. Drizzle over ice cream; top with chocolate pieces. Freeze 1 hour or until firm. Cut into wedges to serve.

FRENCH SILK PIE

MAKES 8 SERVINGS

1 9-inch deep-dish pie crust (frozen or refrigerated)

1⅓ cups granulated sugar

¾ cup (1½ sticks) butter, softened

4 ounces unsweetened chocolate, melted

1½ tablespoons unsweetened cocoa powder

1 teaspoon vanilla

⅛ teaspoon salt

4 pasteurized eggs*

1 cup whipping cream

2 tablespoons powdered sugar

Chocolate curls (optional)

*The eggs in this recipe are not cooked, so use pasteurized eggs to ensure food safety.

1 Bake pie crust according to package directions. Cool completely on wire rack.

2 Beat granulated sugar and butter in large bowl with electric mixer at medium speed about 4 minutes or until light and fluffy. Add melted chocolate, cocoa, vanilla and salt; beat until well blended. Add eggs, one at a time, beating 4 minutes after each addition and scraping down side of bowl occasionally.

3 Spread filling in cooled crust; refrigerate at least 3 hours or overnight.

4 Beat cream and powdered sugar in medium bowl with electric mixer at high speed until soft peaks form. Pipe or spread whipped cream over chocolate layer; garnish with chocolate curls.

GLAZED LEMON LOAF

MAKES 8 TO 10 SERVINGS

CAKE

- 1½ cups all-purpose flour
- ½ teaspoon baking powder
- ½ teaspoon baking soda
- ½ teaspoon salt
- 1 cup granulated sugar
- 3 eggs
- ½ cup vegetable oil
- ⅓ cup lemon juice
- 2 tablespoons butter, melted
- 1 teaspoon lemon extract
- ½ teaspoon vanilla

GLAZE

- 3 tablespoons butter
- 1½ cups powdered sugar
- 2 tablespoons lemon juice
- 1 to 2 teaspoons grated lemon peel

1 Preheat oven to 350°F. Grease and flour 8×4-inch loaf pan.

2 For cake, combine flour, baking powder, baking soda and salt in large bowl; mix well. Whisk granulated sugar, eggs, oil, ⅓ cup lemon juice, 2 tablespoons melted butter, lemon extract and vanilla in medium bowl until well blended. Add to flour mixture; stir just until blended. Pour batter into prepared pan.

3 Bake about 40 minutes or until toothpick inserted into center comes out clean. Cool in pan 10 minutes; remove to wire rack to cool 10 minutes.

4 Meanwhile, prepare glaze. Melt 3 tablespoons butter in small saucepan over medium-low heat. Whisk in powdered sugar and 2 tablespoons lemon juice; cook until smooth and hot, whisking constantly. Pour glaze over warm cake; smooth top. Sprinkle with lemon peel. Cool completely before slicing.

WARM CHOCOLATE SOUFFLÉ CAKES
MAKES 4 SERVINGS

6 tablespoons (¾ stick) butter

4 ounces semisweet chocolate

½ cup granulated sugar

1½ tablespoons cornstarch

⅛ teaspoon salt

2 eggs

2 egg yolks

Raspberry Sauce (optional, recipe follows)

Powdered sugar

1 Spray four 6-ounce ramekins with nonstick cooking spray. Place on small baking sheet.

2 Combine butter and chocolate in small saucepan; heat over low heat until melted, stirring frequently. Combine granulated sugar, cornstarch and salt in medium bowl; mix well. Add chocolate mixture to sugar mixture; whisk until well blended.

3 Whisk eggs and egg yolks in small bowl. Add to sugar mixture; whisk just until blended. Pour batter into prepared ramekins; cover and refrigerate overnight.

4 Prepare Raspberry Sauce, if desired.

5 Preheat oven to 375°F. Bake 18 to 20 minutes or just until cakes are barely set (batter does not jiggle or look shiny). Sprinkle with powdered sugar; serve with Raspberry Sauce.

RASPBERRY SAUCE

Combine 1 (12-ounce) package thawed frozen raspberries and ¼ cup granulated sugar in food processor or blender; process until smooth. Press through fine-mesh sieve to remove seeds.

TOFFEE CAKE WITH WHISKEY SAUCE

MAKES 9 SERVINGS

8 ounces chopped dates

2¼ teaspoons baking soda, divided

1½ cups boiling water

2 cups all-purpose flour

½ teaspoon salt

¾ cup (1½ sticks) butter, softened

½ cup granulated sugar

½ cup packed dark brown sugar

2 eggs

1 teaspoon vanilla

1½ cups butterscotch sauce

2 tablespoons whiskey

1 cup glazed pecans* or chopped toasted pecans

Vanilla ice cream

Glazed pecans can be found in the produce section of many supermarkets with other salad toppings.

1 Preheat oven to 350°F. Spray 9-inch square baking pan with nonstick cooking spray.

2 Combine dates and 1½ teaspoons baking soda in medium bowl. Stir in boiling water; let stand 10 minutes to soften. Mash with fork or process in food processor until mixture forms paste.

3 Combine flour, remaining ¾ teaspoon baking soda and salt in medium bowl; mix well. Beat butter, granulated sugar and brown sugar in large bowl with electric mixer at medium speed 3 minutes or until creamy. Add eggs, one at a time, beating until well blended after each addition. Beat in vanilla. Add flour mixture alternately with date mixture at low speed just until blended. Spread batter in prepared pan.

4 Bake about 30 minutes or until toothpick inserted into center comes out with moist crumbs. Cool in pan on wire rack 15 minutes. Cut cake into nine squares; place on serving plates.

5 Heat butterscotch sauce in medium microwavable bowl on HIGH 30 seconds or until warm; stir in whiskey. Drizzle glaze over cake; sprinkle with pecans and top with ice cream.

CHOCOLATE PEANUT BUTTER PIE

MAKES 8 SERVINGS

10 whole chocolate graham crackers, broken into pieces

2 tablespoons granulated sugar

¼ cup (½ stick) butter, melted

1 package (8 ounces) cream cheese, softened

1 cup creamy peanut butter

1¾ cups powdered sugar, divided

3 tablespoons butter, softened

1¾ teaspoons vanilla, divided

¼ teaspoon salt

2 cups cold whipping cream

½ cup unsweetened cocoa powder

2 packages (1½ ounces each) chocolate peanut butter cups, chopped

1 Preheat oven to 350°F. Combine graham crackers and granulated sugar in food processor; process until finely ground. Add ¼ cup melted butter; process until well blended. Press into bottom and up side of 9-inch pie plate.

2 Bake 8 minutes. Cool completely on wire rack.

3 Meanwhile, beat cream cheese, peanut butter, ¾ cup powdered sugar, 3 tablespoons softened butter, 1 teaspoon vanilla and salt in large bowl with electric mixer at medium speed about 3 minutes or until light and fluffy. Spread filling in cooled crust; smooth top. Refrigerate pie while preparing chocolate layer.

4 Beat cream, remaining 1 cup powdered sugar, ¾ teaspoon vanilla and cocoa in large bowl with electric mixer at high speed 1 to 2 minutes or until soft peaks form. Spread chocolate whipped cream over peanut butter layer; sprinkle with peanut butter cups. Refrigerate several hours or overnight.

ULTIMATE BANANA BREAD

MAKES 6 SERVINGS

BREAD

1¾ cups all-purpose flour

1 teaspoon baking soda

½ teaspoon salt

½ teaspoon ground cinnamon

¼ teaspoon ground nutmeg

2 eggs

3 very ripe bananas, mashed (about 1½ cups)

1 cup packed brown sugar

½ cup vegetable oil

½ cup sour cream

1 teaspoon vanilla

1 cup coarsely chopped walnuts, toasted*

SAUCE AND GARNISH

¼ cup (½ stick) butter

½ cup packed brown sugar

½ cup whipping cream

Pinch salt

2 teaspoons brandy

2 ripe bananas, sliced

¼ cup sliced almonds

Vanilla ice cream or whipped cream

*To toast walnuts, spread on ungreased baking sheet. Bake in preheated 350°F oven 6 to 8 minutes or until lightly toasted, stirring occasionally.

1 Preheat oven to 350°F. Spray 9×5-inch loaf pan with nonstick cooking spray.

2 For bread, combine flour, baking soda, ½ teaspoon salt, cinnamon and nutmeg in large bowl; mix well. Beat eggs in medium bowl. Add mashed bananas, 1 cup brown sugar, oil, sour cream and vanilla; stir until well blended. Add to flour mixture; stir just until blended. Fold in walnuts. Spread batter in prepared pan.

3 Bake 50 to 55 minutes or until toothpick inserted into center comes out clean. Cool in pan 10 minutes; remove to wire rack to cool while preparing sauce.

4 For sauce, melt butter in small saucepan over medium heat. Add ½ cup brown sugar; stir until dissolved. Add cream and pinch of salt; bring to a boil, stirring constantly. Remove from heat; stir in brandy.

5 Cut loaf into 12 slices. For each serving, place 2 slices on plate. Top with sliced bananas, almonds and ice cream; drizzle with additional sauce.

DESSERTS

DOUBLE CHOCOLATE COOKIES AND CREAM MOUSSE

MAKES 8 SERVINGS

8 ounces semisweet chocolate, chopped

2½ cups chilled whipping cream, divided

4 egg yolks

Pinch of salt

1¼ teaspoons vanilla, divided

¼ cup granulated sugar

23 chocolate sandwich cookies, divided

1 tablespoon powdered sugar

1 Melt chocolate in medium saucepan over very low heat, stirring frequently. Remove from heat; stir in ¼ cup cream until well blended.

2 Combine egg yolks and pinch of salt in medium bowl. Whisk about half of chocolate mixture into egg yolks until blended; whisk egg yolk mixture back into chocolate mixture in saucepan. Cook over low heat 2 minutes, whisking constantly. Remove from heat; cool to room temperature.

3 Beat 1¾ cups cream and 1 teaspoon vanilla in large bowl with electric mixer at high speed until soft peaks form. Gradually beat in granulated sugar; continue beating until stiff peaks form. Fold about one fourth of whipped cream into chocolate mixture; fold chocolate mixture into remaining whipped cream until completely combined.

4 Finely chop 2 cookies; fold into mousse. Coarsely chop 2 cookies for topping. Cut remaining 19 cookies into quarters; set aside. Refrigerate mousse 4 hours or overnight.

5 Beat remaining ½ cup cream in large bowl with electric mixer at high speed 30 seconds or until thickened. Add powdered sugar and remaining ¼ teaspoon vanilla; beat until stiff peaks form.

6 Spoon ¼ cup mousse into each of eight wide-mouth half-pint jars. Top with ¼ cup quartered cookies and another ¼ cup mousse. Garnish with dollop of sweetened whipped cream and chopped cookies.

CARROT CAKE

MAKES 8 TO 10 SERVINGS

CAKE

2 cups all-purpose flour

2 teaspoons baking soda

2 teaspoons ground cinnamon

1 teaspoon salt

4 eggs

2¼ cups granulated sugar

1 cup vegetable oil

1 cup buttermilk

1 tablespoon vanilla

3 medium carrots, shredded (3 cups)

1 cup chopped walnuts, toasted

1 cup shredded coconut

1 can (8 ounces) crushed pineapple

FROSTING

2 packages (8 ounces each) cream cheese, softened

1 cup (2 sticks) butter, softened

Pinch salt

3 cups powdered sugar

1 tablespoon orange juice

2 teaspoons grated orange peel

1 teaspoon vanilla

2 cups chopped walnuts, toasted,* divided

To toast walnuts, spread on ungreased baking sheet. Bake in preheated 350°F oven 6 to 8 minutes or until lightly toasted, stirring occasionally.

1 Preheat oven to 350°F. Spray two 9-inch round cake pans with nonstick cooking spray. Line bottoms of pans with parchment paper; spray with cooking spray.

2 For cake, combine flour, baking soda, cinnamon and 1 teaspoon salt in medium bowl; mix well. Beat eggs in large bowl until blended. Add granulated sugar, oil, buttermilk and 1 tablespoon vanilla; stir until well blended. Add flour mixture; stir until blended. Add carrots, 1 cup walnuts, coconut and pineapple; stir just until blended. Pour batter into prepared pans.

3 Bake 25 to 30 minutes or until toothpick inserted into centers comes out clean. Cool in pans 10 minutes; remove to wire racks to cool completely.

4 For frosting, beat cream cheese, butter and pinch of salt in large bowl with electric mixer at medium speed 3 minutes or until creamy. Add powdered sugar, orange juice, orange peel and 1 teaspoon vanilla; beat at low speed until blended. Beat at medium speed 2 minutes or until frosting is smooth.

5 Place one cake layer on serving plate. Top with 2 cups frosting; spread evenly. Top with second cake layer; frost top and side of cake with remaining frosting. Press 1¾ cups walnuts into side of cake; sprinkle remaining ¼ cup walnuts over top of cake.

BROWNIE FIXATION
MAKES 9 SERVINGS

¾ cup (1½ sticks) butter

4 ounces unsweetened chocolate, chopped

1¾ cups sugar

4 eggs

1 teaspoon vanilla

¾ cup all-purpose flour

½ teaspoon salt

Hot fudge sauce

Caramel ice cream topping

Vanilla ice cream

½ cup chopped pecans

1 Preheat oven to 350°F. Line 8- or 9-inch square baking pan with parchment paper or spray with nonstick cooking spray.

2 Combine butter and chocolate in medium saucepan; heat over low heat until melted, stirring frequently. Remove from heat; stir in sugar until well blended. Add eggs, one at a time, beating until well blended after each addition. Stir in vanilla. Add flour and salt; stir just until blended. Pour batter into prepared pan.

3 Bake 20 to 23 minutes or until toothpick inserted into center comes out with fudgy crumbs. Cool in pan on wire rack 10 minutes.

4 Heat hot fudge sauce and caramel topping according to package directions. Cut brownie into nine squares. For each serving, place warm brownie on serving plate; drizzle with hot fudge sauce. Top with ice cream, caramel topping and pecans. Serve immediately.

PUMPKIN CHEESECAKE

MAKES 12 SERVINGS

CRUST

18 whole graham crackers (2 sleeves)

¼ cup sugar

⅛ teaspoon salt

½ cup (1 stick) butter, melted

FILLING

1 can (15 ounces) solid-pack pumpkin

¼ cup sour cream

2 teaspoons vanilla

2 teaspoons ground cinnamon, plus additional for garnish

1 teaspoon ground ginger

¼ teaspoon salt

¼ teaspoon ground cloves

4 packages (8 ounces each) cream cheese, softened

1¾ cups sugar

5 eggs

Whipped cream

1 Line bottom of 9-inch springform with parchment paper. Spray bottom and side of pan with nonstick cooking spray. Wrap bottom and side of pan with heavy-duty foil.

2 For crust, place graham crackers in food processor; pulse until fine crumbs form. Add ¼ cup sugar and ⅛ teaspoon salt; pulse to blend. Add butter; pulse until crumbs are moistened and mixture is well blended. Press crumb mixture onto bottom and all the way up side of prepared pan in thin layer. Refrigerate at least 20 minutes.

3 Preheat oven to 350°F. Bake crust 12 minutes. Remove to wire rack to cool completely. Bring large pot of water to a boil.

4 For filling, whisk pumpkin, sour cream, vanilla, 2 teaspoons cinnamon, ginger, ¼ teaspoon salt and cloves in medium bowl until well blended. Beat cream cheese and 1¾ cups sugar in large bowl with electric mixer at medium speed until smooth and well blended. With mixer running, beat in eggs, one at a time, until blended. Scrape side of bowl. Add pumpkin mixture; beat at medium speed until well blended. Pour into crust. Place springform pan in large roasting pan; place in oven. Carefully add boiling water to roasting pan to come about halfway up side of springform pan.

5 Bake 1 hour 15 minutes or until top is set and lightly browned but still jiggly. Remove cheesecake from water; remove foil. Cool to room temperature in pan on wire rack. Run small thin spatula around edge of pan to loosen crust. (Do not remove side of pan.) Cover with plastic wrap; refrigerate 8 hours or overnight. Garnish with whipped cream and additional cinnamon.

DESSERTS

GIANT CHOCOLATE CHIP WALNUT COOKIES

MAKES 12 LARGE COOKIES

1¾ cups all-purpose flour

1 cup cake flour

1 teaspoon baking powder

¾ teaspoon baking soda

¾ teaspoon salt

1 cup (2 sticks) cold butter, cut into cubes

¾ cup packed brown sugar

½ cup granulated sugar

2 eggs

1 teaspoon vanilla

2 cups coarsely chopped walnuts

2 cups semisweet chocolate chips

1 Preheat oven to 400°F. Line two baking sheets with parchment paper. Position oven rack in center of oven.

2 Combine all-purpose flour, cake flour, baking powder, baking soda and salt in medium bowl; mix well. Combine butter, brown sugar and granulated sugar in large bowl; beat with electric mixer at medium speed 2 minutes or until smooth and creamy. Add eggs, one at at time; beat until well blended. Beat in vanilla. Add flour mixture; beat at low speed just until blended. Stir in walnuts and chocolate chips until blended.

3 Shape dough into 12 mounds slightly smaller than a tennis ball (about 4 ounces each); arrange 2 inches apart on prepared baking sheets (6 cookies per baking sheet).

4 Bake one sheet at a time about 12 minutes or until tops are light golden brown. (Cover loosely with foil if cookies are browning too quickly.) Remove baking sheet to wire rack; cool cookies on baking sheet 15 minutes. (Cookies will continue to bake while standing.) Serve warm.

SWEET POTATO PECAN PIE

MAKES 8 SERVINGS

1 sweet potato (about 1 pound)

3 eggs, divided

8 tablespoons granulated sugar, divided

8 tablespoons packed brown sugar, divided

2 tablespoons butter, melted, divided

½ teaspoon ground cinnamon

½ teaspoon salt, divided

1 frozen 9-inch deep-dish pie crust

½ cup dark corn syrup

1½ teaspoons vanilla

1½ teaspoons lemon juice

1 cup pecan halves

Vanilla ice cream (optional)

1 Preheat oven to 350°F. Prick sweet potato all over with fork. Bake 1 hour or until fork-tender; let stand until cool enough to handle. Peel sweet potato and place flesh in bowl of electric stand mixer. *Reduce oven temperature to 300°F.*

2 Add 1 egg, 2 tablespoons granulated sugar, 2 tablespoons brown sugar, 1 tablespoon butter, cinnamon and ¼ teaspoon salt to bowl with sweet potato; beat at medium speed 5 minutes or until smooth and fluffy. Spread mixture in frozen crust; place in refrigerator.

3 Combine corn syrup, remaining 6 tablespoons granulated sugar, 6 tablespoons brown sugar, 1 tablespoon butter, vanilla, lemon juice and remaining ¼ teaspoon salt in clean mixer bowl; beat at medium speed 5 minutes. Add remaining 2 eggs; beat 5 minutes. Place crust on baking sheet. Arrange pecans over sweet potato filling; pour corn syrup mixture evenly over pecans.

4 Bake 1 hour or until center is set and top is deep golden brown. Cool completely on wire rack. Top with ice cream, if desired.

RED VELVET CAKE

MAKES 8 TO 10 SERVINGS

CAKE

- 2 cups all-purpose flour
- 2 tablespoons unsweetened cocoa powder
- 1 teaspoon salt
- 1¼ cups buttermilk
- 1 bottle (1 ounce) red food coloring
- 1 teaspoon vanilla
- 1½ cups granulated sugar
- 1 cup (2 sticks) butter, softened
- 2 eggs
- 1 tablespoon white or cider vinegar
- 1½ teaspoons baking soda

FROSTING

- 2 packages (8 ounces each) cream cheese, softened
- ½ cup (1 stick) butter, softened
- 6 cups powdered sugar
- ¼ cup milk
- 2 teaspoons vanilla
- 4 ounces white chocolate, shaved with vegetable peeler

1 Preheat oven to 350°F. Spray three 9-inch round cake pans with nonstick cooking spray. Line bottoms of pans with parchment paper; spray with cooking spray.

2 For cake, combine flour, cocoa and salt in medium bowl; mix well. Combine buttermilk, food coloring and 1 teaspoon vanilla in small bowl; mix well.

3 Beat granulated sugar and 1 cup butter in large bowl with electric mixer at medium speed 5 minutes or until light and fluffy. Add eggs, one at a time, beating until well blended after each addition. Add flour mixture alternately with buttermilk mixture, beating at low speed after each addition. Stir vinegar into baking soda in small bowl. Add to batter; stir gently until blended. Pour batter into prepared pans.

4 Bake about 20 minutes or until toothpick inserted into centers comes out clean. Cool in pans 10 minutes. Invert onto wire racks; peel off parchment and cool completely.

5 For frosting, beat cream cheese and ½ cup butter in large bowl with electric mixer at medium speed until creamy. Add powdered sugar, milk and 2 teaspoons vanilla; beat at low speed until blended. Beat at medium speed until smooth.

6 Place one cake layer on serving plate. Top with 1½ cups frosting; spread evenly. Top with second cake layer; spread with 1½ cups frosting. Top with remaining cake layer; spread remaining frosting over top and side of cake. Press white chocolate shavings into side of cake.

RESTAURANT INDEX

RECIPE INDEX

RECIPE INDEX

RECIPE INDEX

RECIPE INDEX

TRADEMARKS

Abuelo's is a registered trademark of Food Concepts International.

Applebee's is a registered trademark of Applebee's Restaurants LLC.

Au Bon Pain is a registered trademark of ABP CORPORATION.

Bahama Breeze is a registered trademark of Darden Concepts, Inc.

Baker's Square is a registered trademark of American Blue Ribbon Holdings, LLC.

Benihana is a registered trademark of Benihana National Corp.

Bertucci's is a registered trademark of Bertucci's Corporation.

BJ's Restaurant & Brewhouse is a registered trademark of BJ's Restaurants, Inc.

Bob Evans Restaurant is a registered trademark of Bob Evans Restaurants, LLC.

Boston Market is a registered trademark of Boston Market Corporation.

Breugger's Bagels is a registered trademark of Breugger's Enterprises, Inc.

Buca di Beppo is a registered trademark of BUCA, Inc.

California Pizza Kitchen is a registered trademark of California Pizza Kitchen, Inc.

Carrabba's Italian Grill is a registered trademark of Bloomin' Brands, Inc.

The Cheesecake Factory is a registered trademark of TFC Co. LLC.

Chili's is a registered trademark of Brinker International.

Claim Jumper is a registered trademark of Landry's Restaurants Inc.

Cinnabon is a registered trademark of Cinnabon, Inc.

Claim Jumper is a registered trademark of Landry's, Inc.

Corner Bakery Cafe is a registered trademark of CBC Restaurant Corp.

Cracker Barrel is a registered trademark of CBOCS Properties, Inc.

Dairy Queen is a registered trademark of AM.D.Q. Corp.

Dickey's Barbecue Pit is a registered trademark of Dickey's Barbecue Restaurants, Inc.

First Watch is a registered trademark of First Watch Restaurants, Inc.

Hooter's is a registered trademark of Hooters, Inc.

Jason's Deli is a registered trademark of Deli Management, Inc.

Joe's Crab Shack is a registered trademark of Ignite Restaurant Group.

Levain Bakery is a registered trademark of Levain Bakery.

Longhorn Steakhouse is a registered trademark of Darden Concepts, Inc.

Maggiano's Little Italy is a registered trademark of Brinker International, Inc.

McAlister's Deli is a registered trademark of McAlister's Corporation, Inc.

Morton's The Steakhouse is a registered trademark of Landry's, Inc.

Noodles & Company is a registered trademark of Noodles & Company.

Olive Garden is a registered trademark of Darden Concepts, Inc.

The Original Pancake House is a registered trademark of Original Pancake House Franchising, Inc.

Outback Steakhouse is a registered trademark of Bloomin' Brands, Inc.

Panera Bread is a registered trademark of Panera Bread.

Pappadeaux is a registered trademark of Pappas Restaurants, Inc.

Pei Wei is a registered trademark of Pei Wei Asian Diner, LLC.

Pollo Tropical is a registered trademark of Pollo Operations, Inc.

Popeyes is a registered trademark of Popeyes Louisiana Kitchen, Inc.

Portillo's is a registered trademark of Portillo's Hot Dogs, LLC.

Potbelly Sandwich Shop is a registered trademark of Potbelly Corporation.

Red Lobster is a registered trademark of Red Lobster Hospitality, LLC.

Romano's Macaroni Grill is a registered trademark of Romano's Macaroni Grill.

Roy's Restaurant is a registered trademark of Roy's Restaurant.

Ruth's Chris is a registered trademark of Ruth's Hospitality Group.

Seasons 52 is a registered trademark of Darden Concepts, Inc.

Starbucks is a registered trademark of Starbucks Corporation.

TGI Fridays is a registered trademark of TGI Friday's, Inc.

Wendy's is a registered trademark of Wendy's International, LLC.

Which Wich? is a registered trademark of Which Wich Inc.

Yard House is a registered trademark of Darden Concepts, Inc.

Zio's Italian Kitchen is a registered trademark of Zio's Italian Kitchen.

Zoës Kitchen is a registered trademark of Zoës Kitchen.

METRIC CONVERSION CHART

VOLUME MEASUREMENTS (dry)

1/8 teaspoon = 0.5 mL
1/4 teaspoon = 1 mL
1/2 teaspoon = 2 mL
3/4 teaspoon = 4 mL
1 teaspoon = 5 mL
1 tablespoon = 15 mL
2 tablespoons = 30 mL
1/4 cup = 60 mL
1/3 cup = 75 mL
1/2 cup = 125 mL
2/3 cup = 150 mL
3/4 cup = 175 mL
1 cup = 250 mL
2 cups = 1 pint = 500 mL
3 cups = 750 mL
4 cups = 1 quart = 1 L

VOLUME MEASUREMENTS (fluid)

1 fluid ounce (2 tablespoons) = 30 mL
4 fluid ounces (1/2 cup) = 125 mL
8 fluid ounces (1 cup) = 250 mL
12 fluid ounces (1 1/2 cups) = 375 mL
16 fluid ounces (2 cups) = 500 mL

WEIGHTS (mass)

1/2 ounce = 15 g
1 ounce = 30 g
3 ounces = 90 g
4 ounces = 120 g
8 ounces = 225 g
10 ounces = 285 g
12 ounces = 360 g
16 ounces = 1 pound = 450 g

DIMENSIONS

1/16 inch = 2 mm
1/8 inch = 3 mm
1/4 inch = 6 mm
1/2 inch = 1.5 cm
3/4 inch = 2 cm
1 inch = 2.5 cm

OVEN TEMPERATURES

250°F = 120°C
275°F = 140°C
300°F = 150°C
325°F = 160°C
350°F = 180°C
375°F = 190°C
400°F = 200°C
425°F = 220°C
450°F = 230°C

BAKING PAN SIZES

Utensil	Size in Inches/Quarts	Metric Volume	Size in Centimeters
Baking or Cake Pan (square or rectangular)	8×8×2	2 L	20×20×5
	9×9×2	2.5 L	23×23×5
	12×8×2	3 L	30×20×5
	13×9×2	3.5 L	33×23×5
Loaf Pan	8×4×3	1.5 L	20×10×7
	9×5×3	2 L	23×13×7
Round Layer Cake Pan	8×1½	1.2 L	20×4
	9×1½	1.5 L	23×4
Pie Plate	8×1¼	750 mL	20×3
	9×1¼	1 L	23×3
Baking Dish or Casserole	1 quart	1 L	—
	1½ quart	1.5 L	—
	2 quart	2 L	—